Unraveling Threads

The Journal Non/Fiction Prize

Unraveling Threads

Essays on Inheritance

brenda Lin

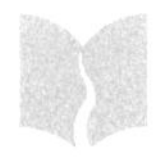

MAD CREEK BOOKS, AN IMPRINT OF
THE OHIO STATE UNIVERSITY PRESS
COLUMBUS

Mad Creek Books, an imprint of The Ohio State University Press.

Library of Congress Cataloging-in-Publication Data
Names: Lin, Brenda (Writer and literary translator) author
Title: Unraveling threads : essays on inheritance / Brenda Lin.
Description: Columbus : Mad Creek Books, an imprint of The Ohio State University Press, [2026] | Summary: "Essays exploring the interconnections between text and textile, interweaving examinations of the author's mother's Taiwanese and Chinese textile collection with themes of belonging, inheritance, motherhood, homecoming, family, and the Asian diasporic experience"— Provided by publisher.
Identifiers: LCCN 2026009703 | ISBN 9780814259887 paperback | ISBN 081425988X paperback | ISBN 9780814284995 ebook | ISBN 081428499X ebook
Subjects: LCSH: Lin, Brenda (Writer and literary translator) | Lin, Brenda (Writer and literary translator)—Family | Textile fabrics—Collectors and collecting—Taiwan | Children's clothing—Taiwan | Inheritance and succession—Taiwan | Homecoming—Taiwan | Taiwanese Americans | Taiwanese—United States | LCGFT: Essays | Biographies
Classification: LCC E184.T35 L63 2026
LC record available at https://lccn.loc.gov/2026009703

Cover design by Charles Brock
Text design by Stuart Rodriguez
Type set in Adobe Caslon Pro

♾ The paper used in this publication meets the minimum requirements of the American National Standard for Information Sciences—Permanence of Paper for Printed Library Materials. ANSI Z39.48-1992.

Once more, for my mother

Contents

Umbilical Cord
繫 1

On Baby Carriers
紅 17

Translation Is a Gift
緣 27

On Characters with the Radical 糸
糸 44

Home
網 57

On Women's Work and Creativity
繡, 織, 編 76

Nationality
絡 85

On Collecting
系統 99

Interstitial Space
紓 116

On Containers and Containment
納 127

Language/Pattern/Writing
紋 145

On Inheritance
繼 165

Mao Dun Things
結 182

Acknowledgments 195

Umbilical Cord

Before my mother's wedding day, my grandmother gifted her the umbilical cord that had dried up and fallen off her newborn belly, which Ama had carefully saved all those years. This is a common practice in Taiwanese families because Taiwanese people love homonyms, and *umbilicus,* which is the navel, is pronounced like the word for *wealth* (臍/財) in Taiwanese. When one's umbilical cord is returned, it is transformed into an ouroboros gift of good wishes. My mother showed hers to me when I was a little girl. The saved umbilical cord was brown and hard, like the carcass of an insect many days after its death. It was strange and it was beautiful. The umbilical cord is what ties a baby to her mother when the baby is nested within her like a Russian doll, wholly dependent, sharing cells, fluids, air. I marveled at the actual purpose of the umbilical cord, the poetry of its thingness. That the connection between mother and child could be preserved, wrapped in tissue, placed into an envelope, and returned as a gift years later—surely, this was a form of magic.

"Where's mine?" I had asked.

"I don't have *ours,*" my mother told me flatly.

I wrote my first book in graduate school, fueled by this hurt. Like most mother-daughter relationships, ours was complex. I had always admired my mother's intellect and discerning eye—she is a collector—which made me thirst all the more for her approval of my creative pursuits. A response she often gave to something I offered: "I'm difficult to please." Our relationship was complex, which in turn made it meaningful.

It should come as no surprise that, in the end, I realized I didn't need the physical umbilical cord to understand that the currents holding me to my mother were not only strong but alive and pulsing with energy. The greatest champion of my book when it was published—simultaneously surprising and obvious—was my mother.

I titled the book *Wealth Ribbon*, a direct translation of the Taiwanese for *umbilical cord*, 財帶, and dedicated it to my mother.

∞

My mother is a textile collector—specifically, handwoven and hand-embroidered children's textiles from China and Taiwan—because she worked for many years at the children's apparel business that my father started in Taiwan in 1971. The business didn't own mills or spin threads, but there were always patternmakers and cloth cutters and seamstresses at my parents' office. Once, when my brother was seven or eight, he was running around in the office, doing flips and cartwheels, and somehow, he got his foot caught in a cloth cutter. One of the men—the company was always overwhelmingly female in demographic—carried my brother and his bloody foot away from the machinery. To this day, he has a scar at the base of his right big toe where the doctor sewed his foot back together. This is how I remember it.

My mother's job was in merchandising, and on her travels for work to Europe and all over Asia, she bought lace, embroidered cotton, silk scarves, batiks, obis, and saris. She conjured ways of stitching these fabrics together to make blouses, jackets, and matching purses. For a time, her signature was to refashion large squares of silk scarves into cap-sleeve blouses with mandarin collars and two Chinese knot buttons at the throat. When communication between Taiwan and China opened up in the late '80s, most of her travel pivoted to China, where she was introduced to the weaving and embroidery practices of minority cultures. She would create her own textile study trips and stay with families in villages in Guizhou, learning about the process of cloth making. The first textile she collected was a Miao baby carrier.

I grew up with the language of textile and tactility:

thread
spinning
fabric
dyeing
weaving
warp
weft
sewing
embroidery
knit
pliability
complexity
give
folding
mending
tying
wealth ribbon

∞

A friend who was newly pregnant had told me that she could feel an actual burrowing in her pelvis. When I became pregnant with our first child, I imagined there was a muffled tapping coming from inside my uterus, like a tiny person was knocking on a tiny little door in a tiny underground house.

I had been an incongruently tall child, the same height as many grown women in Taiwan (five feet) and two whole heads taller than most other kids by the time I was nine years old. While my preadolescent peers were willowy and thin, or sinewy and athletic, I was already soft and curvy. My size and shape felt embarrassing because the timing was so premature. I stopped growing one year later, so eventually everyone around me caught up, then towered over me, the result being that I'd always felt I inhabited an anachronistic body. But pregnancy allowed me to reclaim all the ways my body had once betrayed me. I observed the physical changes—rounded belly, swollen breasts, strengthened legs to support my new weight—with welcome curiosity. Tracking the size of the growing baby, which most pregnancy websites compared to different foods—a poppy seed, a lentil, a blueberry, a fig, then a peach, a sweet potato, a grapefruit, a pumpkin, and finally, a watermelon—made me feel of this earth, like I was rooted and was growing, sprouting from humus, and that I belonged exactly in this body, where my baby fruit was planted inside.

When I was six months pregnant, we traveled to San Francisco for a cousin's wedding. It happened to be my thirtieth birthday, so a few nights before the wedding, my family made plans to gather at the pizza place where we used to go when my mother, brother, and I lived in the Bay Area. We had lived there for four years—along with most of our extended family—while my father was setting up his business in Taiwan.

Before our pizza dinner, my mother presented me with a birthday gift, which was a very odd gesture, because we didn't grow up with the habit of birthday gift giving. At six months, the baby was the size of a large grapefruit. I felt the grapefruit shift, push up against the walls of its house, as if the baby were trying to reach for this gift. My mother handed me an old US passport. The words *Bicentennial 1776–1976* were embossed on the cover. I opened it to the first page and found a picture of a newborn baby with its swollen eyes sealed shut, being held up by a man wearing a maroon sweater with the name ERIC in cream lettering on one sleeve. The man's face and legs were cut off so that the focus was on the baby. I recognized the sweater; it was my father's, a sweater my mother had knit for him when they were in graduate school. I didn't recognize myself. I fingered my typewritten name and birth date, as though they were Braille. Then, something fell from the pages of the passport: a small, yellowed envelope. I shook out its contents into the palm of my hand.

"It's your umbilical cord," my mother told me.

∞

Two thousand years before the modernist notion that things are the carriers of the ineffable—"no ideas but in things"—the Chinese philosopher Zhuangzi wrote about the oneness of all things in the collected chapters titled 齊物論. The most common translation of 齊物論 is "the equality or myriad of all things," which proposes the idea that all things—both animate and inanimate—are united through their inherent spirit. Tangible things hold the weight and meaning of the human condition—concrete things tell stories; material things harbor emotion. We are interconnected not because human beings are poetic and create those connections, but because all things are equally poetic and therefore already intertwined in a delicately balanced web of thingness.

The 齊 in 齊物論 can also mean "together." When the radical for *flesh,* 月, is added to 齊, the character 臍—*umbilicus*—is created.

∞

My mother *had* saved our umbilical cord. She'd simply forgotten where she had kept it and was embarrassed to admit she might have lost it, so she allowed me to be angry with her. I think she trusted that I would eventually understand that the thing itself did not matter.

> *Matter,* from the Latin *materia*—"timber," "substance," or "subject of discourse." *Matter* also comes from *mater*—"mother."

My mother was right—when I didn't have it, the umbilical cord had become this beautiful metaphor for the tie between mother and child, between a person and her place of origin. Now that I possessed the actual umbilical cord and could hold this metaphor in the palm of my hand, the spirit of its utilitarian purpose was palpable and electric. I looked down at my hardened, lopsided belly, with the grapefruit pushing insistently against my uterus, and felt the presence of the umbilical cord that, at that very moment, was transporting all the nutrients and all the knowledge in my physical body to the grapefruit so that it could grow into a coconut by next week.

Later that evening, we drove to the pizza place to gather

with family. We had printed out directions from MapQuest, but they lay unused on the dashboard. Instead, we used my mother's memory as a guide. This was the route she used to take to drop my brother off at school, to drop me off at Fan Tai Tai, or the babysitter's, and finally, to get to work at the lab for half the day before driving the same stretch of freeway in the opposite direction to pick us up. How many countless times had she traversed this route, going back and forth between leaving us and being reunited with us, this palimpsestic loop of emotions (heartbreak, relief, joy) that tethered her to her children? As we drove down this short stretch of freeway, I listened to my mother recount the mundane yet wonderfully nostalgic details of her daily routine thirty years ago and felt the road beneath us metamorphose into a ribbon, which linked us to the ever-widening reaches of our past.

∞

Anni Albers was one of the leading textile artists of the twentieth century. In her book *On Weaving*, she laments the diminishment of our collective tactile sensibility—specifically, that while our articulation of thought through reading and writing had become more sophisticated, our sense of touch had become dulled. And yet, she writes, "We touch things to assure ourselves of reality. We touch the objects of our love. We touch the things we form." I imagine she is warning that if our tactile sensibilities are blunted, our ability to express love may be compromised. Therefore, if we sharpen our sense of touch, broaden the vocabulary of our tactile sensibilities, then the things we touch will feel that love, and we can reawaken the inherent spirit that lives within all things.

∞

Pregnancy had returned me to my body, but this time, in a doubled existence. I was aware of the little toes and appendages growing in my body, of the elbows and shoulders and a row of bones along a back I would one day smooth with the warm palm of my hand as I shushed into the shell-like ear of the baby to lull him to sleep. I felt that every part of my physical body was necessary and useful and needed. It was finally the right body at the right time.

The bulk of my first pregnancy was spent in Singapore, where my husband, Billy, and I had just moved from New York. We had moved for Billy's job, while I was trying to write what I hoped would be another book; we didn't know a single person in Singapore. I spent most of that pregnancy by myself exploring a new city, buying furniture for our apartment, reading and eating snacks, not really writing. I was alone, but I was never lonely. The baby inside kept growing and making its presence known. One night, the baby shook vigorously, making the skin on my belly—now pulled taut over his growing figure inside—quiver and spark like millions of raindrops against pavement. It was an exhilarating dance of life, and I placed my hands on the rounded curve of my large abdomen, reabsorbing the energy that came from the little being inside back into my hands, into my body.

For the last month of pregnancy, I temporarily moved to Taipei to stay with my parents and prepare for childbirth and for zuo yuezi, the traditional Taiwanese practice of "sitting the month" after the baby is born to allow mothers' bodies to recuperate and recalibrate postpartum. This month is known as the fourth trimester and is just as important as the three trimesters of pregnancy. My mother was semiretired then but kept a busy schedule, into which I was folded. She was intent on keeping me active and constantly moving, bringing me along everywhere she went: to the wet market, to swim laps at the pool, to Chinese calligraphy class, to lunches with aunties who were eager to share their stories of pregnancy and sitting the month. In my journal from that time, I often wrote about how tired I was, keeping pace with my mother. But I didn't want to refuse her invitations. The way I remember it is that when I was young, my mother wasn't interested in playing with me. In a way, my pregnancy returned me to her; she regarded the physicality of my pregnancy with amusement, as if she were experiencing it for the first time. She didn't want me to be still or separate from her. Now, I see that the baby and I were not merely doubles, but along with my mother, we were a tripled—a braided—existence.

> *Complex*, from the Latin *com*—"together," and *plex*—"to braid."

∞

Toward the end of forty weeks, the baby was still in a breech position, so when I went into labor, I had to have a Cesarean birth. Billy made it from Singapore, just in time. He sat next to me, near my head, in the operating room. The epidural made my teeth chatter, and it was difficult for my mouth to form words. Billy smoothed the hair back from my forehead; his hand felt warm and big and in control. I watched his face as he looked back and forth between me and what was happening in the lower half of my body.

And then suddenly, "I see him! I see him!"

I let go just a little. My teeth continued to clatter in my head, like loose marbles rolling around on an unsteady plane. I looked at Billy's still smiling face, his eyes glistening. And then we both heard it, the piercing cries of our baby boy, loud and insistent and, somehow, already confident. My shakes melted into cries; tears rolled down Billy's cheeks and into the creases of his smile.

That first night in the hospital, I still couldn't feel the bottom half of my body and was afraid to move my legs, which were leaden from the epidural. Before and during the surgery, I had started to shake uncontrollably, my body humming with an energy that didn't feel like it was coming from me, but now, there was a weight. The nurses brought the baby in whenever he was hungry; I would open up my hospital gown, and when they set him down on my chest, I realized the weight I was feeling was him, the physical reality, the real responsibility I had of him. When the baby started rooting and suckling, it was astonishing and exciting and overwhelming. I had no idea what I was doing—I felt like I had been doing this for years. I drifted in and out of sleep, dreaming that my breasts were like larger-than-life Georgia O'Keeffe flowers dripping milk off their smooth petals. At one point during this thick, velvet night, I began wondering how I would make it out of the hospital, how I would make it off the bed, how I would detach the catheter and the IV dripping pain medication into my vein? How would I make it out of this dark hospital room, where I wanted to stay forever with my baby in the confident care of the nurses, and all the way back to Singapore? I can worry, especially late at night when time yawns ahead into a vertiginous space, and this was the same, except now there was this little being whose life very literally depended on my being able to care for him. So I held on—breathed and focused on the moment, and then only as far as what I needed to do the very next moment, which was to close my eyes and rest until the next time the baby came in to nurse.

∞

As planned, I did my yuezi in my parents' home after the baby was born. In Taiwan, the tradition is steeped in the tenets of Chinese medicine; it's a time when the mother eats specific yang foods to balance out the overabundance of yin—associated with the moon, coolness, and female elements, such as childbirth—in her body. I stopped eating meat when I was fourteen years old, but as soon as I became pregnant, my body craved the sinewy texture and bloodied juices of meat. During the yuezi, I ate six times a day—pork knuckles stewed with peanuts to bring on milk, chicken cooked in ginger and rice wine to bring up the temperature in my body, leafy greens with red veins to replenish my blood, and snacks of sweet red bean soup with chewy glutinous rice balls floating in the bowl to increase caloric intake, because, the yuezi nurse explained, breastfeeding used up calories quickly. Between meals, I nursed my baby and performed pelvic and abdominal exercises. The yuezi nurse laid me down on my bed and told me to push my finger into my belly button. Astonishingly, my finger kept on sinking into the softness of the space my newborn recently vacated. The nurse said this was where my abdominal muscles had separated to make room for the baby, and the exercises would encourage them to fuse back together again.

For one month, I didn't leave my parents' apartment; I rarely even left the bed. A friend who had her first child a year before I did wrote in her congratulations card, "Enjoy the newborn cocoon!"

We lived in an apartment in downtown Taipei after we left San Francisco when I was four. My mother started working at my father's company; I remember often crying hysterically before she left for work. The lighting in that apartment was always dark. My brother was already in grade school, and that first year back in Taiwan, I spent most of my time at home with an elderly housekeeper we called Obasan, so with just the two of us in the apartment, we didn't turn on many lights. One day, my mother brought home a shallow cardboard box. Inside were large green mulberry leaves and a handful of soft and squishy white silkworms. I peered into the box and watched them inch across the carpet of leaves, all the while nibbling voraciously. The silkworms were pudgy and not unpleasant to look at. In the quiet of the apartment, I thought I could hear them chomping on the mulberry leaves. Two or three days later, when I checked inside the box again, the leaves had been consumed and mulched, and the silkworms were gone. In their place were silk cocoons that looked like tiny ovals of dragon whisker candy, which is made from thinly spun sugar. I don't remember what we did with the cocoons or if we let the moths hatch. My mother told me that the cocoons were made with one single strand of silk, that for those two to three days, spinning silk around and around their own bodies was all the little worms did.

In the room where I was sitting the month, I performed the singular job of caring for this little being who had so recently been housed inside my body. For four weeks, we stayed cocooned in that room, where I imagined I was spinning a glossy strand of silk around our bodies, soft and wispy like cirrus clouds brushed across a blue sky. Billy was on paternity leave and staying with me at my parents' place, in the room they always kept for my grandmother when she visited. The room and everything in it made up my entire universe of existence for four weeks.

I did nothing but nurse the baby and marvel at his impossibly tiny fingernails and feel the smooth, pristine bottoms of his feet that knew nothing yet of weight or friction. I had no desire to leave the room and relied on my mother for everything we needed. She brought us diapers and nursing pads, and when one breast threatened mastitis, she filled a sock with dried adzuki beans and warmed it in the microwave for me to press on the lumps of clogged milk ducts, coaxing them to soften under the heat. When I ran out of blank nursing logs—which I was diligently filling out with information like the baby's temperature, which breast I nursed from at what time and for how long—my mother was the one who made copies for me. She brought all my yuezi meals and snacks, studying the recipes with the attention of a student preparing for college entrance exams. My mother has often said that in another life, she would like to be a traditional Chinese doctor. She was our connection to the outside world. It was as if I had been returned to her womb, and we were once again connected by a 臍帶, one through which she delivered everything the baby and I needed.

∞

In "Material as Metaphor," Albers writes,

> A short while ago I had a visit from [a] 10 week old baby who looked at me wide eyed and I thought somewhat puzzled and was struggling as if trying to tell me something and did not know how.
>
> And I thought how often did I feel like that, not knowing how to get out what wanted to be said.
>
> Most of our lives we live closed up in ourselves, with a longing not to be alone, to include others in that life that is invisible and intangible.
>
> To make it visible and tangible, we need light and material, any material.

For Albers, her material was thread and, more specifically, the tactility of threads when woven together in a coded sequence. In order to break through from the quiet, cocooned existence of our minds, we need material that we can touch and mold, material that can translate the interiority of our experience. In order to sharpen our tactile sensibilities, so that we can deepen our vocabulary for love (Albers, again: "We touch things to assure ourselves of reality. We touch the objects of our love. We touch the things we form."), we need material.

The materials in my yuezi cocoon: nursing logs, a belly band I was told to wear during this month to encourage my internal organs to come back together, little squares of muslin cloth we put over our shoulder when we burped the baby, socks filled with dried beans, nursing pads, a baby carrier for when we were ready to bring the baby outside.

And the baby himself—the baby who was nestled inside me and who was now out in the world, with skin I could touch, eyes I could look into, whose tiny, warm breath I could smell, and whose delicate heartbeat now pulsed to its own rhythm—the baby was now matter.

∞

When the baby was manyue, "one month old," the three of us would return to Singapore and begin our life as parents in earnest. A few days before our departure, when I was nursing the baby, I felt something—a small particle—roll off of him and onto the bed. Thinking it was some kind of lint, I looked for it with the intention of throwing it away until I saw what it was—his umbilical cord, dark brown, dried up, and hard. I rolled it around in my fingers and looked into my baby's face. He looked older, I decided. I laid him down on the bed, and he squirmed helplessly, making gurgling noises, jerking his clenched fists here and there in the air.

When my mother showed me her umbilical cord, I was a little girl—younger than ten. I understood in a general way that I had stayed in my mother's belly for nine months before emerging into the world, but the logistics of how I lived, housed inside and underwater, was not something I had considered. My mother's umbilical cord was physical proof of the biology of nascent motherhood, and, never having been a scientifically inclined child, the tactile thingness of this phenomenon seemed utterly magical to me. What I was sure of were the intangibles—the fact that I was fiercely connected to my mother with invisible strands of admiration and longing, that I wanted to be close to her, and that I yearned for her approval. That this yearning came from a physical ribbon that once tied us together as one was breathtaking and astounding. And now I held in my hand the thing that had fastened my baby to me, the conveyor that carried information, nourishment, and my deepening love for him. Would he one day understand and feel the weight of this metaphor?

I rummaged around the room and managed to find a little plastic bag, dropped the umbilical cord into it, and tucked it into my journal on the writing desk. The desk was covered with things I hadn't had a chance to put away since coming back from the hospital: pamphlets on breastfeeding, a list of foods to avoid in the first month, the baby's and my hospital bracelets, his immunization record, and among them, his birth certificate, which my mother had brought home a few weeks ago. Even this documentation of the baby's existence—material proof of his being—was delivered by my mother. She was the conveyor of all the things we needed before we nibbled our way out of the silk strands of our cocoon, before we made our own way into the world.

Is part of the complexity of certain mother-daughter relationships in the ultimate knowingness of the mother's position?

What I often read—and still read—as judgment or withholding on her part was perhaps her waiting for me to arrive at a conclusion she already knew. For example, that I didn't have to be hurt when I believed my mother didn't save our wealth ribbon. Parenting requires an inordinate amount of quiet patience; my mother didn't have to explain because, eventually, I came to this realization on my own. She could wait. And it meant so much more that I experienced this revelation in my own time. The fact that this thing that didn't matter—the umbilical cord between me and my mother—had materialized, had literally mattered itself back into how I related to my mother, shifted my understanding of the metaphor once again. Everything we feel—everything we metaphor in order to comprehend—resides in tangible things.

∞

I had decided to birth my baby in Taiwan because we were on our own in Singapore and I wanted to sit the month under my mother's care. It was a decision I made for me, less for my baby. But when I read the words *Born in Taipei, Taiwan* on his birth certificate, it made my heart swell to see that my son came into this world on this island, this home I loved but had, until then, no intention of returning to.

I don't remember feeling it, but there must have been, at that moment, a gentle tug on the cord that tied me to home.

On Baby Carriers

紅

My mother is a collector.

Growing up, we traveled a lot as a family, mostly to countries near Taiwan. Always, my mother found a pocket of time in our itinerary to disappear into the local market, befriending people who had the willingness and patience to show her interesting local handicrafts and antiques. On the occasions I trailed along with her, I saw my mother—who usually played the role of quiet introvert next to my garrulous father—most in her element, her eyes glistening with excitement as she wound her way through dusty alleyways and gesticulating animatedly with shop owners and artisans, her hands eagerly brushing against the grooves in ancient and handmade wares, wanting to learn about each piece. As she collected these varied artifacts from our travels—everything from lacquered boxes to leather shadow puppets to tiffin boxes to old land deeds—she was, like an anthropologist, collecting stories about a particular culture and its people.

In my memory, my mother was always studying something in her free time. After a day of work at my father's children's-apparel company, where she headed the merchandising department, my mother would take language classes at the local university—French for a time, and then Japanese. On Sundays, when my father was out playing golf or mah-jong, I would find her at her desk, poring over some big book, underlining passages, and making margin notes. The topics varied; often, it would be about Chinese art and sculpture or traditional Chinese medicine. She went through a wine phase, too, studying the wine-making regions in France. Later, I learned that a clairvoyant friend of hers had told her she had been a vineyard owner in her past life. I wondered if, when reading up on the wine regions in France or about the wine-making process, she experienced something akin to déjà vu, which, because she had taken French classes, she pronounced in a respectful French accent, pursing her mouth into a tight O, like she was preparing to whistle, so that *déjà vu* rhymed with 魚 in Chinese. My mother was a zoology major in college and continued her graduate studies in biological sciences. She learned things in a methodical, thorough way.

When my mother talked to artists and craftspeople at bazaars and markets, she asked questions that proved her curiosity was genuine. Buying things as souvenirs is different from procuring things to build or add to a collection. The impetus for the former is superficial and topical; the inspiration for the latter is deep, even urgent. My mother wanted to learn about the techniques, the materials used, the traditions, and the stories. Her openness and willingness to absorb these stories was moving, and her excitement was infectious. It was not uncommon for shop owners and artisans to excuse themselves into back rooms and reemerge with that rare piece they weren't willing to part with until now, having met my mother, this passionate collector worthy of owning their pièce de résistance.

One day many years ago in an antique shop in Hong Kong, my mother chanced upon an intricately hand-embroidered piece

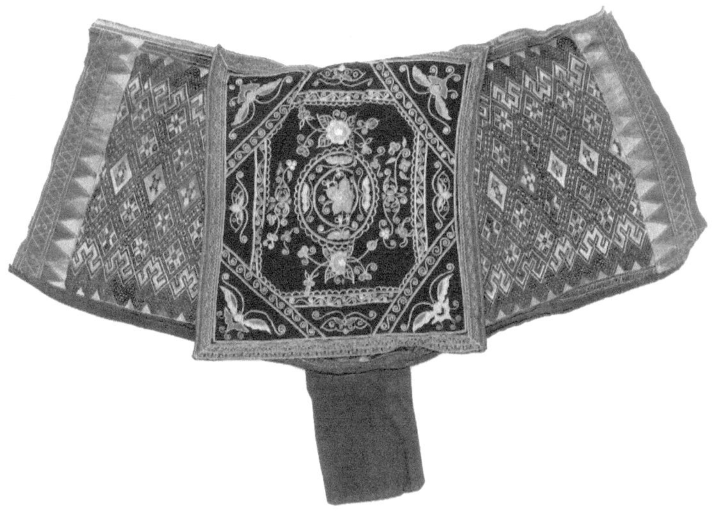

of rectangular cloth, which dramatically changed the course of her collecting. This piece of cloth, she explained to me, was the main body of a baby carrier that was handmade about eighty years ago by a mother from the Miao minority tribe of China. The deep, dark blue of the velveteen cloth was dyed using plant extracts indigenous to the rolling hills of the southwestern region of China where most Miao people reside. Threads of once-vibrant yellows and magentas were woven into the cloth in impossibly minute stitches, forming geometric shapes that twisted and turned into dizzying optical illusions. A smaller flap, embroidered with curlicues and butterflies and flowers and flowers that bloomed into butterflies, lay over the bottom piece.

My mother told me this version of the Miao origin story: A felled sweet gum tree in the forest transformed into a beautiful Butterfly Mama. Butterfly Mama was lonely and flitted to the river, where she fell in love with a water bubble and, together with the water bubble, laid twelve eggs. Because Butterfly Mama

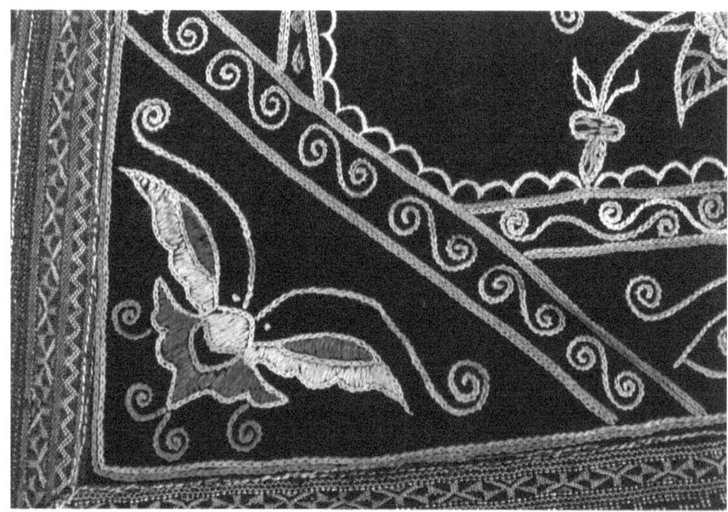

couldn't sit on the eggs to hatch them, she enlisted the help of the qitu bird, who could warm the eggs until the creatures inside were ready to peck their way out into the world. The twelve creatures that Butterfly Mama created were a dog, a tiger, a mountain cat, a centipede, a snake, a chicken, a ram, an ox, an elephant, a dragon, thunder, and finally, a human being. That is why butterflies are such an important motif in Miao embroidery—Miao people believe they are direct descendants of Butterfly Mama. How at odds this strange and fantastical story was to my mother's science mind! But when I interrupted her story with questions, she looked at me with disapproval and disappointment: How could I *not* get that butterflies and water bubbles could mate and give birth to eleven creatures plus one weather phenomenon? Perhaps it was my mother's science background that gave credence to this origin myth; because I knew her mind to be logical, I softened into the magical folds of the story.

Back to the baby carrier. It was simultaneously delicate and sturdy. The bottom layer was thick and had weight to it, but my mother could also see that this heft had been softened with use and time. At first glance, she wasn't sure if it was woven or embroidered, but she could see that multiple techniques were employed: Appliquéd pieces and stitches inched along the edges in diamond patterns, reinforcing the borders. Examining it closely, she could see the thickness varied where threads doubled, sometimes tripled, in the embroidered areas, like a paintbrush loaded up with more paint to make thicker gestures on a canvas. The bottom layer was in the general shape of a rectangle, but it curved ever so slightly because of three darts gathered at the top. It was easy for my mother to imagine that the curvature at the top was put in so that the carrier could wrap the little baby's body more snugly. The piece that flapped over the bottom layer, my mother realized, must have been purely for decorative purposes, as it was simply an embroidered panel. Perhaps it could have been flipped up to cover the baby's head, as sun protection? But flipping the panel up would have revealed the underside of the embroidery, the reverse of the images on the front side, with frayed knots where threads were snipped and tied. In truth, there was something beautiful about seeing the backside of this panel. My mother learned that, by examining the reverse side of an embroidered piece, she could tell whether it was hand or machine embroidered. Confirming that this was, in fact, embroidered by hand, stitch by achingly beautiful stitch, filled her chest with a mixture of awe and respect and sadness—sadness, because she knew this kind of handiwork was quickly giving way to machine work.

The butterflies were the anchor motifs of the baby carrier. They represented the Miao origin story, and the geometric shapes on the side panels represented the flora and fauna of the region, specifically, the octagonal anise flower, which is a symbol of abundance and life. Baby carriers were sometimes made by the maternal grandmother, but in this case, my mother was told, it was made by the pregnant young mother, who was preparing for her baby's imminent arrival. My mother imagined this young woman carefully planning out the design of the baby carrier, stitching the stories of her culture's becoming, and filling the fabric with wishes of plenty for her child. The Miao aesthetic is that more is more in the design and use of motifs as well as in the variety of embroidery techniques; the abundance of all these facets ensures abundance in a baby's future, like an explosion of life and dreams and possibilities.

My mother was deeply moved by the expression of this young mother's love for her unborn child—her physical labor in anticipation for her baby, all the hopes she had for it that she stitched into the fabric. When she relayed the story of this baby carrier to me, her eyes became glassy. I puzzled over how the baby carrier worked without straps or ties. She explained that, when this mother parted with her baby carrier—by then, all her children were grown, and she was likely selling her baby carrier to an antiques buyer for some extra cash—she cut off and held onto the ties, which, though worn threadbare, were, more importantly, the metaphorical umbilical cord between mother and child; the ties, despite being physically cut, exemplified the emotional bond between mother and child that could never be severed. Because Miao women carried their babies all day, every day, they believed the baby's spirit was infused in the cloth of the carrier, and when the baby had outgrown her carrier, the straps were saved to protect the child's spirit. Some mothers performed rituals—burning or burying the straps—to shelter the child's soul.

Because of this baby carrier, my mother started to travel to rural parts of China in search of more in order to understand more viscerally the embroidery techniques and the stories behind each motif. (She described staying with a Miao family on one of her trips and finding a black boar slumbering in the corner of their outhouse!) She was fascinated by the culture of textile making, which she viewed as rich and strong and in many ways radically feminine. In many minority Chinese cultures, girls are taught from a young age how to harvest cotton, spin thread, weave and dye fabric, and finally, to embroider images and stories onto that fabric to make all the textiles that a family would use: clothing, shoes, hats, blankets, bags, tablecloths, toys. In most cultures around the world and throughout history, cloth making is women's work. (The Chinese character for *needlework* is made up of the radical for *thread* and the character for *labor*, 紅.) It's repetitive, soft, and domestic as opposed to the masculine activities of hunting and staking new grounds, outbound exploration, the hardness of warfare. My mother saw how cloth making was the physical representation of caretaking, which is made even more significant when the cloth is adorned with female script that recorded a culture's history, as well as a particular family's hopes and dreams. And nowhere was this confluence of tactile care and memorializing more physically embodied than in the baby carriers she collected.

∞

I have another theory about my mother's fascination with baby carriers. My mother says she has no memory of ever being carried by her own mother. My grandmother was the main breadwinner of the family, an ophthalmologist who ran her own eye clinic on the first floor of the house my grandfather built in the city of Taichung. My mother was the second of five children, born at the tail end of the Second World War. The family lived above and behind the clinic, so most of the caretaking was done by nurses and helpers, as well as my mother's Hakka grandmother on her father's side, who my mother describes as a stern, well-dressed woman you did not want to mess with. My mother doesn't fault Ama for not having had the time to carry her when she was little; in fact, that she was never carried is the start of the story about Ama's greatness, about the exceptional circumstance of her being a female doctor in Taiwan during Japanese occupation and after, when Chinese Nationalists took over the island. Not only was she a female doctor who sustained her family and her artist husband, her work had real, tangible effects in the community, such as bringing trachoma medicine into schools and seeing patients who had slivers of metal stuck beneath their eyelids from working in nearby mines. Years later, she would become the ophthalmologist who brought contact lenses to Taiwan.

I believe my mother when she says she doesn't resent the fact that Ama was too busy to carry her, especially considering the way women from that time carried their babies; they wore them in cotton slings around their backs or hanging off their fronts like baby sloths, and still they went about the daily labor of caring for the family—leaning over chopping boards, squatting in the courtyard to do the washing, wading in the shallow waters of paddies to plant rice in pencil straight rows. But I do think my mother yearns for the tactile memory of being carried. Perhaps, in a way, we all do. I don't have memories of my mother carrying me, either, though I have seen photographs of us when we lived in California and I looked to be the size of a rice dumpling and my mother had me pinned to the ledge of her hip or slung over her shoulder after I'd fallen asleep at some family function where various knee-high cousins crowded around the adults' legs. Maybe my mother had been carried by Ama, but she had simply forgotten, and she didn't have the photographic proof that I have.

Maybe it is a function of our still-developing brains in the first few years of life that we forget what it feels like to be held by our mothers, so that we spend the rest of our lives reaching for that memory, reaching for our mothers' soft, embodied love that feels primal and whole because it exists outside of language or logic. (Could some of us in the habit of reaching for that forgotten tactile memory of being held transpose that yearning into a constant desire for approval?)

And so I think my mother's fascination with baby carriers is born from this tactile amnesia. Even if her introduction to textile collecting was unintentional, she grew into her role of merchandising manager at my father's children's-apparel company seamlessly, and, now into her identity as a collector of children's textiles logically and with ease. Textile collecting seemed to give her daily work purpose. Studying the history and making of children's textiles from various cultures grounded her daytime responsibilities in the otherwise merely transactional business of children's apparel retail. And collecting baby carriers, specifically, reconnected her to her primal maternal relation to the world.

It is a gross understatement to say that you won't understand your parents until you become one yourself. When my mother began her baby-carrier collection, I was in graduate school, already dating my husband but still very much in the mindset that parenthood was something in the amorphous and distant future. A woman's place in the world changes dramatically the moment her body houses another life, another soul, and delivering that once-physical part of her into the world is a lifelong lesson in humility and in letting go. Now that my baby is born, I feel a constant tactile urgency, a need to be close to him, to hold him against my chest so that I need only bow my head down to breathe in his tender scent of sleep, to brush my lips against the

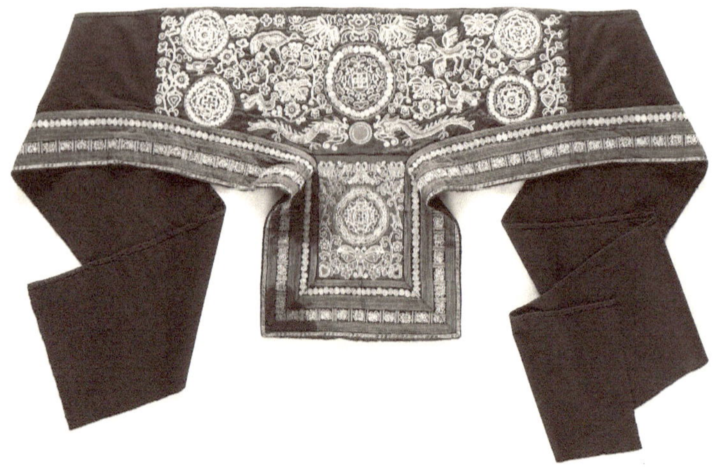

downy softness of his scalp. Even when he is not in my arms, my body continues to respond to his needs the way it did when he was still in utero—automatically, without thought. He will be sleeping in the next room, and my breasts will tingle and fill with milk and soak the nursing pad *before* he cries out in hunger. We are still viscerally connected, and this tactile urgency is my body's animal response to our very recent separation. That he will one day forget we were once so inextricably tied is a certainty.

Memory is the technical term used by textile conservators to describe the wrinkles imprinted in garments from repeated wear, the scents from one's body that cannot be fully laundered and forgotten from its fibers. If we can anticipate this tactile amnesia of being carried by one's mother, then the memory housed in baby carriers is all the more singular and magical. Like the umbilical cord that dries up and falls off a newborn baby and can be dropped into an envelope for years of safekeeping, the baby carrier, too, is both metaphor and actual thing that embodies that metaphor and elevates the idea back to the wonder of its thingness.

Translation Is a Gift

緣

The first word I translated from Mandarin to English for my husband was 緣. We had met on a summer study-abroad program in St. Petersburg, Russia, during White Nights, when, at the end of each day, the sun dipped below the horizon, just grazing the night, before it glided back up into the sky, and we felt as though time belonged to us. Or, maybe it was that we felt we belonged outside the borders of time. We were bright-eyed twenty-year-olds, newly philosophical and contemplative but also wild and brazen. Billy was foreign to me, as I must have been to him—he had grown up in San Diego and had never eaten fried rice; I had grown up in Taiwan and was afraid to swim in the ocean. But there was a tethering that was happening. And before the end of our St. Petersburg White Nights, before we returned to opposite coasts of the US, where we attended our respective colleges, I needed him to know what I knew—that this tethering was the red thread of yuan.

I translated, gently pulling him across the threshold between languages. 緣 is not a sentence like fate or an arrow like destiny, both of those concepts having a linear, unidirectional connotation.

In fact, one of yuan's homophones is the word for *round.* Yuan has to do with past lives, in whatever form, and can exist between living beings, with objects, and places. 緣 has something to do with karma and cosmic alignment. With each description, I expected Billy to look at me with suspicion, or for my translation to sound feathery and exotic. Neither happened. He seemed to get it right away, and I felt I was bearing the meaning across with appropriate gravity and complexity.

The magic of translation happens when the space between languages is made smaller. In translating 緣 for Billy, I felt the space between us diminish. This act of bearing across was less like laying down a plank to bridge a gap, but more like a piece of cloth folding gently in on itself. Chinese characters are usually made up of two parts—a radical, which denotes the root meaning of the word, and a character part that hints at its pronunciation or deepens its meaning. Characters with the radical 糸 on the left side of the word—as in 緣—have to do with silk, cloth, thread, or weaving. In addition to being a homophone for the character for *round,* yuan is also pronounced the same way as the word for *border,* which is why the word 緣 is also used to describe an ornamental border on clothing.

In fact, I did feel that we were dancing on the border of something that summer, but, instead of being hurled outward, we were circling in.

∞

The first time my mother invited me to write a book with her was for a translation project that also included my grandmother. This was her idea: Ama, my mother, and I were all to write short essays in the language of our education—Japanese, Mandarin, and English, respectively—and then, like a translation version of the birthday party game, Pass the Parcel, we would give our writing to my mother. My mother would then translate Ama's Japanese and my English into Mandarin before handing her translations to us, so that Ama and I could translate each other's words into Japanese and English, because Mandarin was the lingua franca of the three generations, the linguistic center that held together recent Taiwanese history.

My mother was putting together a book about her collection of baby carriers from China and Taiwan. Magazine-quality photos of her collection would be accompanied by explanations of the cultural and ethnic groups the baby carriers originated from, descriptions of the embroidery techniques, and the symbolism of particular motifs. My mother's writing tends to have an anthropological tone because of her science background; she likes to simply allow the history and facts surrounding an object relay its inherent beauty. For example, she can identify where a certain baby carrier is from by looking at its shape, material, the colors of its dyes, and the arrangement of the embroidered motifs. Most of the baby carriers in her collection are from minority tribes or Indigenous cultures in China and Taiwan, societies without a written language and for whom embroidery *is* the mode of record. My mother taught me that, in Chinese, embroidery is referred to as 女書, "female script," without which there would be no tactile record of myths and origin stories. Sometimes, fact alone can be poetry. The essays Ama, my mother, and I wrote were interspersed throughout the book; our translated pieces were meant to be the adornment, the 緣, in the original sense of the word, "the decorative border of a garment." But our stories of being mothers and being mothered intermingled in the three languages, the emotional fibers twisting and meshing, and became the net that held the rest of the book together.

∞

The study of gift exchange was first explored in the Western world by French sociologist and anthropologist Marcel Mauss, whose work *The Gift* was published in 1925. Through studying the gift culture of tribal groups in Polynesia, Melanesia, and the Pacific Northwest, Mauss presented the basic structure of gift culture, which is based on three obligations—the obligation to give, to receive, and to reciprocate. Gift giving establishes relationships, especially in small communities. In 1979, Lewis Hyde wrote a book by the same name, extending Mauss's thesis and applying it to art and creativity. Hyde's premise is that art is a gift. He draws on folktales that feature gifts, using them as an integral part of his argument, and illustrates one of the properties of gifts, which is that when they are kept in motion—either by gifting to another person or consuming them—their inherent value increases. One important aspect about this perpetual motion is that the gift moves in a circle, always returning and passing back through its home, back to its source.

My parents did not read to me when I was little. The stories they shared were from their own childhood. I adored listening to them, but my parents weren't the ones from whom I learned about traditional myths and folktales. When my children were born, and my parents became grandparents, I witnessed a softening—the way my mother cradled my babies and sang to them as she looked into their faces, a physical intimacy I have often felt my own childhood lacked—or perhaps it was the memory of being held that I yearned to remember. When my oldest was a toddler, and we were still living in Singapore, I flew home to Taiwan to spend time with my parents; on that visit, my mother told him the story of Momotaro-san, the baby born from a giant peach. I listened, rapt—both because it was my first time hearing the Japanese folktale and because I realized my mother was, in fact, a wonderful storyteller.

The tale of Momotaro-san, my mother's version, as told to my son in Mandarin:

> Once upon a time, there was an old, childless couple who lived in the woods. One day, when the old grandma was washing clothes by the stream, a very, very, *very* large peach tumbled down the current and onto the shore by her pile of laundry. The old grandma was so excited by this peach she hurried home to tell her husband and told him to come quickly. The old grandpa ran to the stream and saw that what his wife said was true. He hoisted the giant peach onto his shoulder, and the old couple walked home in wonderment at their good fortune. When they got home, the old grandpa brought out a large knife and cut into the giant peach. The fruit immediately split into two, and at the center of the fruit was not a large pit, but a ruddy-faced, chubby baby boy. The old couple held each other and wept with joy. They finally had the child they had always wanted. They named the child Momotaro. In Japanese, *momo* is "peach"; *taro* is "firstborn."
>
> The old couple doted on Momotaro-san. He was a pleasant and docile child and treated his parents with respect. He grew quickly, and the family soon realized that not only were his origins mysterious and fantastic, he was also bestowed with superhuman strength. When Momotaro-san was a young boy, news spread across the local villages that there were awful demons, known as oni, up on the mountain, threatening to descend to terrorize the

villagers below. Immediately, Momotaro-san volunteered to hike up the mountain to fight against the oni. Even though the old couple did not want to send their only child into danger, they were also proud of Momotaro-san's courage and willingness to protect the villagers. With a heavy heart, the old grandma packed her little boy a bag of rice balls, and the old couple held their son and wept, pleading for him to return home safely.

On his way to the mountain, Momotaro-san was approached by a talking dog, who kept eyeing Momotaro-san's bag of rice balls, complaining of his empty belly. Momotaro-san hesitated, knowing that he only had a limited supply of his mother's food to get him up the mountain to fight against the oni, but he also took pity on the hungry dog. So Momotaro-san proposed that he share one of his rice balls with the dog in exchange for his help to fight the oni. The dog eagerly agreed and, after finishing the delicious rice ball, trotted alongside Momotaro-san in the direction of the mountain. Soon, the boy and the dog were approached by a talking monkey, who kept eyeing Momotaro-san's bag of rice balls, complaining of his empty belly. Momotaro-san offered the monkey the same arrangement, and after the monkey was satiated, the boy, the dog, and the monkey continued onward toward the mountain. Not long into their journey, the three travelers were approached by a talking bird, who was also hungry, and the same promise was exchanged as Momotaro-san handed over his last rice ball. Finally, the four companions—the boy, the dog, the monkey, and the bird—made their way up the mountain, where they found the band of oni. With their bodies nourished by the old grandma's rice balls, Momotaro-san and his new friends successfully defeated the oni and triumphantly returned to the village.

Momotaro-san went back to his home in the woods, where he and his parents lived together in happiness and peace.

∞

The first time the labor of translation made me weep was when I translated an essay my father had written. It was titled, "Growing Pains." He had written it a month after dropping me off at college. He wrote about how, when he was little, he couldn't wait to become an adult so that he could be independent and free. He writes, "When our car left the university parking lot, leaving our daughter there, waving goodbye to us, my heart did not feel carefree and my tears betrayed me. Could this be the freedom and ease of adulthood I had been yearning for?" In fact, our parting that day was also a moment I had written about in my first book, and though his writing precedes mine, I didn't know his essay existed until recently. I also recalled, in great detail, how their car rolled away from me—I wrote about not being able to see through the windshield as the car backed out, so my parents' faces were obscured by the reflection of the trees overhead. This moment had been pressed, hot, into my memory because the year that followed was an intensely lonely one for me. And now, reading—then translating—my father's essay so many years later felt like I was passing through that pane of glass so that I was sitting beside my parents as they watched my figure become smaller and smaller. It was a rare moment of confluence—like time was being origami-ed.

I wept as I translated my father's writing because I felt—with acute awareness now that my oldest child is seventeen and his imminent departure is often on my mind—that as parents, we must suffer our worries quietly. Freedom in adulthood is a misconception. If, to be Buddhist, we need to part with our attachments to relieve our suffering, then I choose to be tethered to my children, to let my tears betray me, alone inside the car.

∞

Gift giving is a big part of Taiwanese culture. Historically, the two main occasions for gift giving are the Mid-Autumn Festival, a celebration of the fall harvest and the full autumnal moon, and the Lunar New Year, the period of time when the old year is swept out and the new welcomed in. In both cases, the gifts that are exchanged are consumable (either edible or usable): mooncakes, turnip cakes, fish, and red envelopes filled with crisp new bills. The social structure of Taiwanese society is based entirely on relationships, in which gift giving plays an integral part. Gifts are given to extended family, friends, teachers, bosses, doctors, and work colleagues to solidify one's relation with each. Of course, there is a negative side to gift giving, which involves pressure and burden, but, for the most part, Taiwanese people are a generous people who genuinely delight in gift giving. Today, gifting is not limited to just the Mid-Autumn Festival and Lunar New Year. Gifts are exchanged all the time. It is so customary to show up with something to give that, on the occasion you do arrive empty-handed, you can instead offer this joke: Lift up your hands with fingers pointing down and shake them to and fro while saying that you've brought two bushels of bananas with you (note how, even in this joke, the gift of bananas is consumable). And not only should you show up with a gift, if you are the host, you should send your guest off with something to take away—boxed up left-overs count. I have a friend who always has to send me off with something, often grabbing whatever is on her dining table. From this friend I have received, while I had one foot out the door: a chocolate bar, a tube of hand cream, a bar of soap, a bag of chips, a blank journal, a glass vial of powdered incense. Whenever I leave my parents' house, my mother will pack me fruits and vegetables, savory scallion pastries, cartons of eggs, sweet custard bakery buns, rice, even her own take-out leftovers to bring home to my children. Even though Taiwanese people are always in the habit of gifting each other consumables and sending people off with something more to eat or use, we rarely give each other things like birthday presents, as is customary in the West. On the occasion when I have received a present from family, it is significant.

The first book I received as a gift from my parents was a *Merriam-Webster's Collegiate Dictionary*. They gave it to me when I was seventeen, as I was about to leave Taiwan to go to college in the US. The hard cover was dark blue and the pages thin and crackly like garlic skin, and the edges of the book were mottled with mold. The original receipt was still taped to the inside back cover; it had been bought in Hong Kong in December of 1957. I used this dictionary all throughout college and graduate school. Looking up words in the dictionary has always held a sense of magic for me—that the meanings of words can be so precise and full and fit so snugly next to other words and strung together to make sentences, and those sentences woven together to make a story! It feels important that I received a book of words and their meanings from my parents before I left home for New York to study literature and writing, a world so different from the one I had grown up in—especially because, when I left, I had no intention of returning home. In fact, the longer I stayed away, the closer I moved toward home in a strange, inverse trajectory. Distance and time had initiated my internal homing device.

The first Chinese book my parents gifted me was a collection of short essays about the Taoist philosopher Zhuangzi. The inscription from my mother reads, in her feathery Chinese script: "Your father and I have benefitted so much from this book. We hope you can read it slowly, carefully. Hope it will be of use to you." They gave it to me two years into my return to Taiwan. When I left, I was seventeen; when I returned, I was thirty-seven and had come back with Billy and our three young children. I was still just starting to learn how to be at home again as an adult—how to live and work in Mandarin and Taiwanese. Basic things like shopping at the wet market, going to the bank, setting up our cable, liaising with our landlord, and paying electricity and water bills were challenging not just on a cultural level but on the most surface, linguistic, logistic level. On one of my first trips to the bank to set up an account, I had forgotten how to write some elementary characters and had to push an old receipt under the plexiglass window to ask the teller to write it out for me on the back. How could I read a book on Taoist philosophy if I couldn't yet communicate well enough to fulfill the bottommost layer of Maslow's needs? I flipped through the book, the lines of characters blurring into rows of smudgy ink, haphazardly slipped in a random photograph as some kind of marker, and pushed it into a space on my bookshelf, hoping that my parents wouldn't ask me what I thought of Zhuangzi.

∞

The first work of literary translation I performed was a book of essays about homecoming and language and borders by an Indigenous writer in Taiwan. The writer, Apyang Imiq, had grown up swimming in the streams and hiking up and down the mountains of Taiwan's east coast without being taught the language of his tribe, and after years away in Taipei, he realized he did not feel at home in the city, in the language of his colonizer. He writes about farming and hunting and working the soil of the land of his ancestors, he writes with heart-aching honesty about the challenges of asking to be let in, of doing the work to be in. He wrote his book in Mandarin.

I didn't notice how much of my Mandarin and Taiwanese I had lost during my years of absence until I came back and heard how stupid I sounded each time I opened my mouth to speak. I sputtered, garbled, tangled my native languages and resorted to English to complete sentences, which sounded like a betrayal. Reading and writing in Chinese proved even more difficult. I felt deeply embarrassed. When Imiq returns to his native Hualien and starts to farm, neighbors walk by and scoff at his greenness, offering advice and ridicule. He works for hours in the sun, his back in spasms as he crouches over to dig his fingers into the soil, feeling its material weight and texture and moisture and possibility as he nestles seeds into the land, rooting.

I grew up in downtown Taipei in the '80s and '90s in the rapid speed of time-lapse videos one can watch on city planning and construction. In the twenty years I spent away from Taiwan, I lived in cities even more intense in their urban spirit and busyness than Taipei—first in New York, then Singapore, then Hong Kong. I have always loved living in apartments and high rises, knowing that I shared a wall with strangers, simultaneously in close proximity to and welcomed distance from other people's lives and stories. Spending time in nature was never a big part of my upbringing, nor did I yearn for it to be. So I did not expect to be moved by detailed descriptions of farming and the physical labor of working the land. I was fascinated to learn about the process of turning soil, and how many fists Imiq had to leave between each divot when planting millet, the grain of his Truku ancestors. His labor in homecoming laid bare the ways I was not working hard enough to return home. I had arrived, but only insofar as an address change; I still needed to figure out the linguistic, cultural, historical, and emotional coordinates of home. I wanted something akin to digging my fingers into the soil, something that felt like I was sinking into the loamy softness of the mud, reaching out my arms and legs to make angels in the soil.

I say I performed the translation of Imiq's book because it was so much more than a language exercise, so much more than simply replacing an English word for its Chinese counterpart, because the mathematics would not have worked out, as there is no direct counterpart. Translation is an interpretive dance, speaking in another person's voice, moving through the world by way of their gestures. There is an intense becoming that happens, a settling into, a rooting down. And all of this action occurs in the liminal space between languages.

I performed this labor of translation alone at my desk for no purpose other than to nestle in that space where I didn't have to apologize for my lack or my excess in any language, where being neither/nor—but also and, and, and—felt just right. It was how I could root. "To translate" is 翻譯; 翻 is "to flip," "to turn," as one does with soil.

∞

According to Marcel Mauss, in order to keep the spirit of a gift alive, the gift should circle back to its source "to bring to its original clan and homeland some equivalent to take its place." In the story about the boy and the giant peach, Momotaro-san gifts his rice balls to the dog, monkey, and bird, and in turn, each gift's value increases in the form of their friendship and loyalty, as well as by nourishing them to be able to defeat the oni. Ultimately, Momotaro-san returns home to his parents, the original rice balls having long been consumed, but now they have been transformed into Momotaro-san's continuing presence in his parents' life at home. Momotaro-san's return closes the circle of the gift of his mother's rice balls.

The premise of Lewis Hyde's *The Gift* (itself an extension of the original gift of Mauss's book by the same name) is that an artist's creative spirit is a gift. Laboring in the details of craft and the tools of their artistic trade is part of the practice, but artists are humbled by the fact that there is a creative spirit much more powerful than the physical work of doing, a spirit that they are sensitive to and accustomed to channeling. Artists work in solitude and for nothing more than to commune with their gift. But then there comes a moment when they feel compelled to offer their gift to an audience because the gift must be kept in motion so that it may retain its spirit. Hyde quotes the author May Sarton, writing, "There is only one real deprivation, I decided this morning, and that is not to be able to give one's gift to those one loves most. . . . The gift turned inward, unable to be given, becomes a heavy burden, even sometimes a kind of poison. It is as though the flow of life were backed up." A gift must be shared—if it is hoarded, its spirit dies in solitude and silence.

Creativity is shared, in the most obvious way, in public with an audience that appreciates the artist's work—as in a painting that is displayed or a piece of writing that is published. But to go further than that, the creative gift should be able to make its way home, to close the circle the way Momotaro-san, having fought off the oni to protect his village, returns home to his parents. Artists will often acknowledge and direct the spirit of their gift back to its source—be it geographical, familial, or spiritual. Pablo

Neruda has said that his gifts were bestowed upon him by his people, and to honor that gift, he writes, "I have attempted to give something resiny, earthlike, and fragrant in exchange for human brotherhood." We tend to think of the creative spirit as something willowy and ethereal, elusive and diaphanous, when in fact it springs from earthly material—the mossy softness of soil, the hard determination of seeds, the alertness of cool river water, the warmth of a mother's touch.

∞

In his 1921 essay "The Task of the Translator," German philosopher Walter Benjamin proposes the idea that translation is itself a creative mode rather than merely a mechanical tool. Translation is the closest form of reading, and for many writers who are also translators, the most intimately they can come to know the spaces between languages, the meaning making that occurs beyond language, is through translation. Through the act of translation, we can experience the interconnected tissues between languages, flickering and vibrating with life and the energy of renewal. The language with which Benjamin writes this essay—which I read in a translation by Harry Zohn—is magnificently maternal and life-affirming, as words and phrases like these show:

> embryonic, continued life, maturing process, renewal, mother tongue, birth pangs, ever-renewed, abundant flowering, nature, kinship, interrelated, afterlife, creation, posterity, fruitful, seed, nucleus, eternal life, a constant state of flux . . .

Hyde's book *The Gift* is separated into two sections—the first discusses the tradition and practice of the gift economy in different cultures and in folktales, while the second applies this practice to the gift of the creative spirit. A quick scan of the first few pages of the second section on the gift of creativity produces these words:

> *materia,* body, creative, energy, flow, fruit, renewal of spirits, fertility of nature, fertility of the imagination, womb, labor, the thread of zoe-life, relationship, bonding, transformation, everything in the poem happens as a breathing . . .

It should not come as a surprise that Lewis Hyde is a poet and a translator.

∞

For my grandmother's ninetieth birthday, my mother gathered the short essays Ama had submitted to *Pinzette,* the periodical published by her classmates from the Tokyo Women's Medical University, and translated them from Japanese into Mandarin, collecting them into a slim volume. *Pinzette* is the German word for *tweezers,* an instrument that all doctors depend on; the journal's title is in German because most of the medical texts my grandmother used at that time in Japan were from Germany.

The bulk of Ama's essays were written after she had retired from being a doctor for close to fifty years and was living in San Francisco, reveling, for the first time, in homemaking. "Each day," Ama writes, "I enjoy quiet conversations with my husband of fifty-three years, with whom I still have endless things to discuss about life. Recently, we dined while relistening to 'Chinese Art History' on cassette tape—it was the most extravagant and elegant feast for the heart."

In the collection are essays on cooking, her travels with my grandfather, acupuncture (which Ama practiced alongside ophthalmology), naming her youngest grandchild, childhood snacks, movie reviews, Buddhist philosophy, losing my grandfather, attending my brother's college graduation in Ithaca, and suffering a bone fracture in her left wrist. The list reads like Sei Shōnagon's *The Pillow Book*: occasional ponderings on seemingly mundane, everyday things—everyday things that glisten like the amber surface of tea in a tiny ceramic cup, each detail a gift.

Ama writes (translated from Japanese to Mandarin by my mother, which I've translated into English):

> I like to cook (especially three-minute meals), often trading recipes with my group of old friends here; sometimes, I make extra and share with young people who work and don't have time to cook; being able to do housework, work my muscles a bit, I pass the days feeling fulfilled and happy.
>
> After retirement, my journey in Buddhist philosophy began in earnest, I have a deep interest in reading sutras and interpretations of the sutra from the wise, and I try each day to put Zen theory into practice.
>
> I am so thankful for this time in retirement when I can savor "being myself," I don't force myself to do things beyond my capabilities, I feel it is a true blessing to be an ordinary person!

My mother published this volume of essays as a gift to her mother for her ninetieth birthday, gifting the book to family, friends, and of course to Ama's medical school classmates—to whom the essays were addressed for publication in *Pinzette.*

Benjamin says that translation is a mode. I think translation is a gift. Like a creative gift, it begins with a body of work, and through the performative act of translation, the original work is infused with new energy and flow. A translation transforms, but it also returns the creative spirit to the original, circling back to its source. This is something physical that happened to me when I was translating my mother's translation of my grandmother's essays. By gathering up the folds of the fabric of language, I felt as though I were reaching across to hold my mother's and my grandmother's hands; or, it was as though we were nested inside one another like a linguistic Russian doll. If a female baby is born with all the eggs she will ever produce in her lifetime, does that mean that when my mother was still in my grandmother's womb, I was there, too, as a follicle of the future? And does that mean, when I was still physically bound to my mother by our umbilical cord, the promise of my future daughter already glowed inside my mother's belly like a little bag filled with stars from the night sky?

∞

I remember once watching my mother trim Ama's toenails—Ama sat on a step of her carpeted stairs, while my mother sat a few steps below, cradling Ama's outstretched foot in her hands. By then Ama's feet were perpetually swollen and the skin around her ankles transparent, revealing the complex web of blue vessels underneath. My mother held Ama's foot in the palm of one hand, as one might hold up the head of a baby when her neck is still too weak, and with her other, she confidently clipped Ama's nails. Ama caught my eye and smiled, a mixture of mild embarrassment and pride. "Your mother is so good," she said to me.

What gift will I give my mother? If mothers are the original source of one's creative gifts, what can I return to her? Will I be able to take her swollen feet in my hands and translate the pain into the gestures of love?

On Characters with the Radical 糸

Chinese characters are formed with a radical that indicates something about its meaning, then it's combined with another character or character root that either gives a hint about its pronunciation or, together with the radical, deepens its meaning. Characters that contain the radical 糸 have to do with silk and threads. The oldest form of Chinese writing was carved into the backsides of turtle shells or the bones of large animals, such as oxen, more than three thousand years ago. The radical 糸 was originally written like this:

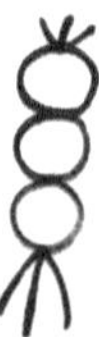

It isn't difficult to see this as a rendering of a piece of knotted string—with thread represented by the three strands at the top and bottom and the two loops in the middle as two knots in the string—that either forms the foundation chain for a piece of knitting or perhaps the intertwining of threads to make rope. There are over 150 characters with this radical, which means there are over 150 words that have to do with thread. For example:

紅 (hóng)

The color red.

The radical for *thread* on one side and the character for *work* on the other forms the character for *red,* which also means "women's work," such as spinning, weaving, dyeing, and embroidery.

練 (liàn)

To cook raw silk, hemp, or cotton until it becomes clean and ready to be spun into fibers.

This is a multistep process, which is why, in modern parlance, 練 means "to practice by doing something over and over again."

經 (jing)

Warp threads.

These are the threads that run vertically on a loom, the static plane onto which weft threads, which run horizontally, are passed through, creating the woven patterns, the script of the weaving, the meaning it is trying to convey.

經 also means "to pass through," "to experience." When coupled with the moon, 月經 is "menstruation." 經 can also mean "scripture," which is likely derived from the Sanskrit word *sutra,* which originally referred to string or thread before it evolved into the word for "religious script."

紙 (zhǐ)

Paper.

Paper is made by softening strips of tree bark, soaking and cooking them until they are clean—the process of 練—and then beating the paste to create the desired length and thinness of fibers to weave together to create a strong plane with a certain tensile integrity and pliability. After the woven plane is wrung out of moisture and dried, it becomes a surface on which to write, draw, and paint.

The paper used for copying the heart sutra in Chinese

calligraphy is called 宣紙. It is thin and porous, soft like cotton. My mother uses a form of this kind of paper, which is acid-free and gentle, to wrap her textiles and cushion the storage bins, laying thin pages between baby carriers and baby blankets and little tops and pants. The paper protects and helps absorb unwanted moisture. Sometimes we find dried up carcasses of dead insects nestled in the fabric or on the bottom of the storage bins.

結 (jíe)

Knot, both as a noun and a verb.

Pre-language, the Chinese used to tie knots on a string as a mnemonic device to note an event. 結 can mean "to come together," as when tying knots on a string to form a rope; it can mean "to wed, to marry."

結 in Buddhism also refers to the nine knots, or disturbances of the heart, such as jealousy, greed, anger, pride, stupidity, and doubt.

My parents never asked me or my brother to come home. But they wanted us to. That must be a knot of the heart too.

組織 (zǔzhi)

But I did come home to Taiwan.

Organization.

Warp and weft threads on a loom were the first form of binary coding. At its most basic, fabric is made from the constant, alternating over-under of weft threads passing through the vertical warp plane. This interlocking of threads forms the strong foundation of all fabrics and is an organizational system that lays the groundwork for textiles that not only clothe us and keep us warm, but that hold and contain things, and are the sails upon which years of naval exploration depended. We often forget how integral to civilization textiles are—and not only as material but as an analogy for community. 組織—"organization," which combines the word for *group* 組 and the word for *weave* 織—has become a ubiquitous business term. Companies begin with an organization chart, the most intricate of which can almost read like a weaving pattern.

I grew up with the language of textiles, characters with the radical 糸, because apparel retail was the industry in which my parents worked. But I also grew up with the language of textiles because my father was an entrepreneur, and textile language forms the basis for business culture and organization. He spoke often about 系統, "systems," and 績效, "efficiency"—three of these four characters are anchored with the radical for *thread.*

When I was a kid, before I became vegetarian, I shared my dad's penchant for Taiwanese food that made use of the whole animal—pig's blood, pig intestines (which he called Chinese chewing gum because we could nosh on its bouncy, elastic texture for minutes at a time), chicken heads and necks, and ox tails. My dad and I would go eat at little stands and noodle shops, and as we ate, he was constantly calculating how many customers came in, how much money they spent, what leftovers they tended to leave behind, how many people the stalls employed, how much rent that particular area may charge. He made note of the systems these tiny shops used to efficiently serve their customers and applied his findings to his own business. Taiwan in the 1980s was an entrepreneur's dream playground, ripe with opportunities and promise.

But neither textiles nor business interested me, so I went off—carrying the dictionary my parents had gifted me—to study English and Russian, then writing, believing that my trajectory was to hurtle outward, to spiral farther away from home in order to figure out who I was on my own. But then one day, without my realizing it, my internal homing device clicked on.

網 (wǎng)

Web, net.

Spiders come up a lot in my mother's textile collection. Spiders are considered an auspicious animal because they have eight legs, and eight is a significant number—there are eight trigrams in Taoism, eight fairies who traverse across the seas in Chinese mythology, octagonal flowers like azaleas in Miao embroidery that signify abundance. Spiders are also regarded as highly intelligent and crafty creatures because they can spin silk and create intricate webs. I've observed spiders moving in space, suspended in an invisible plane, working all eight of their legs in different capacities while extruding silk. What mechanism do spiders possess to have the spatial awareness to know the exact distance between the spokes of their webs, to draw in space the geometry of radii and anchor points? Do humans have a similar internal homing device? Is that what brought me back home?

In Singapore, we put our eighteen-month-old in a day care across the street from our apartment for a few hours a day so that I would have time to write. In the space for emergency contact, we put our neighbor's information. When our son turned two, we decided to move to Hong Kong, where my brother and a few cousins lived. We wanted to be able to put down the name of a family member in the space for emergency contact.

Spider webs are both a home and a trap. The part of the character 網 that tells you how the word is pronounced is nestled inside; one hardly notices it. It is 亡, which means "death."

But then the very aspects of home I tried to resist helixed into the twin threads that eventually pulled me back: my mother's textile collection and my father's apparel business. I returned home to Taiwan after a twenty-year absence and began to work in

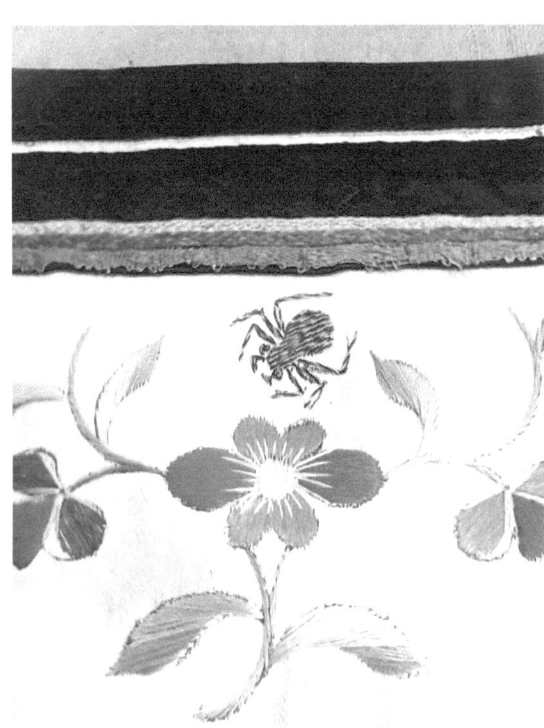

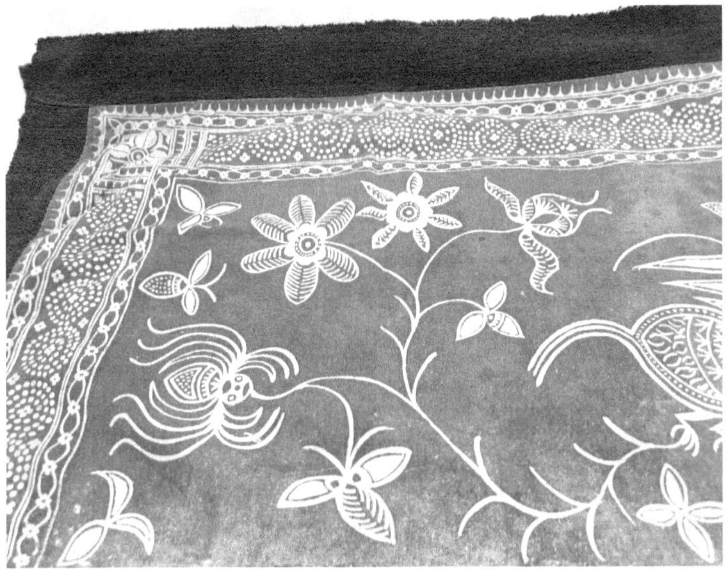

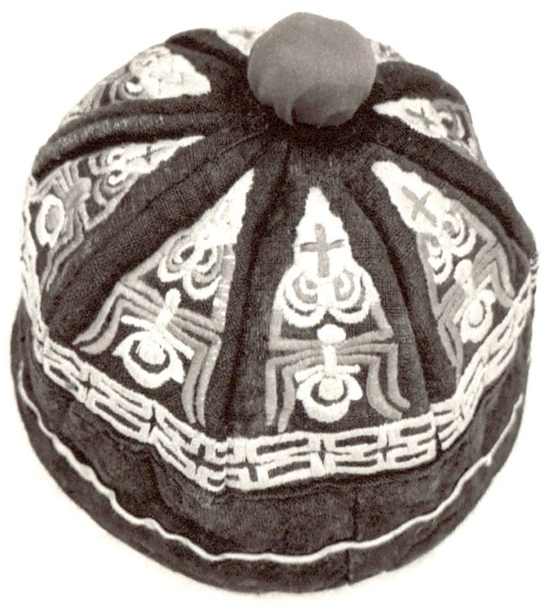

the family business not because I had any interest, but because I thought I was performing the role of an obedient, filial Taiwanese daughter.

繡(xìu), 織(zhi), 編 (bian)

Embroider, weave, create.

The same was true with the translation work I did for my mother, which began when I was still in graduate school in New York, years before my return home. My mother's writing on her textile collection would arrive in big manila envelopes from Taiwan, and I would translate her technical writing into English for the books she wanted to publish on her textile collection. I translated for my mother from a distance and learned the terms of women's work (繡, 織, 編—*embroidery*, *weaving*, and *creating*) before ever coming into physical contact with the textiles themselves. When I was still in New York, I was too self-involved with my own writing endeavors, and translation felt like a chore. I was a passive helper to my mother's project, viewing myself as merely a technical conduit between languages. But even as I resisted, I was obedient and completed my homework.

When I moved back home to Taiwan, I started to spend time with my mother's textile collection. We unrolled baby carriers from between layers of paper and laid them out on desks, and my mother explained how certain stitching, embroidery, and weaving techniques gave clues to where a piece was from. My eyes crawled across the textiles, my head dizzy from the tiny stitches, the arrays of colors, the stories of origins and magic and abundance told through motifs and symbols. It made me want to do something with my hands too.

I went to an embroidery class where the teacher described French knots as cream puffs with dimples and urged us not to flatten them. She referred to individual threads as though they were people. For example, she said, "If you pull from the skein of embroidery floss and the thread gets tangled, you may wonder to yourself, 'What happened to him? How come he didn't make it out with the others?'" I befriended a young woman who owned a yarn shop and bought balls and balls of yarn in colors like wine, cream, lake, and lime and admired the shawls and cowls and socks she knit with delicate needles that clacked together like fingernails on a pane of glass. She invited me to feel a spool of yarn that had been spun from sheep so recently, our fingers smelled like a cold, wet Scottish barn and had the thin residue of oil from lamb's wool. I took a weaving class from a young Atayal weaver who named her studio 不老東東. The last two repeated characters are pronounced "dong dong" to mimic the sound the weaving shuttle makes as the weaver strikes the last woven line to make for a tighter, more uniform weave.

紓緩 (shu huǎn)

To relieve, slow down.

In an interview with the poet Jorie Graham I once listened to, she talks about the souls of tools that have been passed on, the histories and memories embedded within its substance, how inherited tools bear the weight of time. She then makes a reference to paintings and etchings of women sewing and weaving, saying that the scenes depict quiet, persistent work that was quiet because the hands that were at work *were* the minds.

Being able to feel my mother's textiles, the weight of the fabrics, the bumps and grooves of the embroidery, the smooth satin finish of the stitches—there was an energy that I wished to understand and inhabit and become. What Graham describes as the synergy between the work and the mind, that is what I want. That is what I found when I followed the thread home.

What I experience when I stitch is bodily—my heart rate decreases, my breath slows, my mind stills, and I settle into this traditional craft of female script.

絡 (luò)

Fibrous network in fruits and vegetables, veins, context.

The complex pathways that connect mind and body—neural networks and veins and connective tissues—all of those ribbons of information help form the context of larger meaning; every stitch, every weave creates a larger narrative fabric.

紋 (wén)

Pattern, text.

Text is derived from the Latin word, *textus,* which means "tissue, literary style, or woven"; the root is both *text* and *textile.* All this time, I was searching for a sense of self distinct and far away from the world my parents had woven together—my father's apparel business, my mother's textile collection—only to find that the thread I've followed—writing—has not only brought me back home, but that it is made of the same connective tissues of *warp* and *weft,* of *organization* and *pattern,* of *practice* and *creativity.*

In *On Weaving,* Anni Albers writes about the interconnectivity and organization of threads as an expressive medium, a tactile language that technology and mass production threaten to gloss over and efface. The second half of the book contains photos of looms, tapestries—her own and artifacts—examples of draft notations, which are plotted designs of weavings blocked out on graph paper, and studies of what she calls "tactile sensibility" using different materials, such as grass, metal shavings, twisted paper, and corn kernels.

Plate 41 (shown on the next page) takes my breath away. It is a study made on a typewriter. Rows of repeated punctuation—opening and closing parentheses and underscores—in a pattern that resembles weaving on a loom.

See how the parentheses undulate like strands of hair, like waves, like currents?

繼 (jì)

To continue, inherit.

Look at all those 糸s! It is like an Albers study in miniature.

My mother encourages me to write about her textile collection. She no longer needs me to translate for her, but she wants me to take over her collection and write about it. I want to and I don't want to.

I have stopped buying new clothes and have begun wearing my mother's hand-me-downs. It is like the idea of the children's clothes in her collection but in reverse. Whereas traditional handmade children's clothes were adorned with symbols of hope and promise, I am wearing remnants of my mother's experiences, her memories, her missteps and triumphs. Who am I in her clothes?

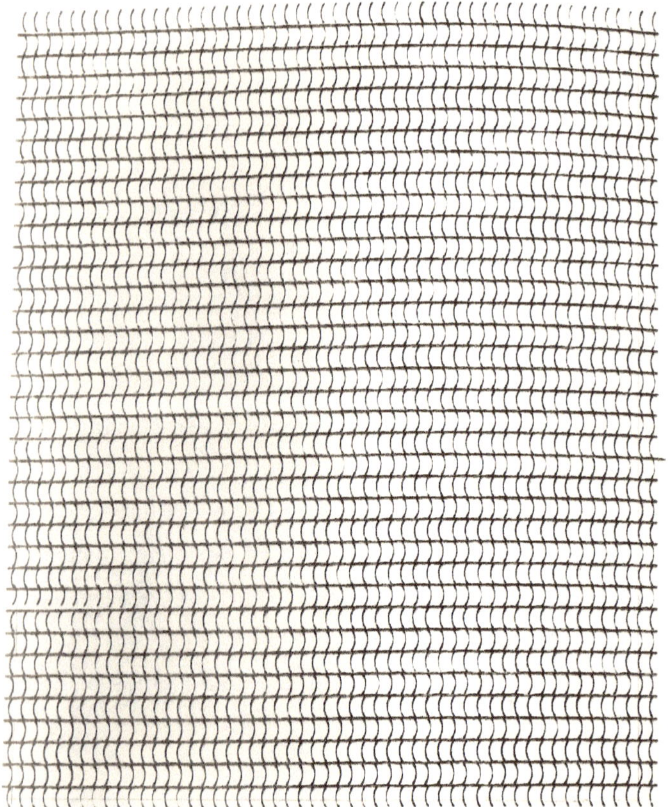

Plate 41. Study made on the typewriter.

By dressing in her clothes, am I physically inhabiting the cliché of becoming my own mother? When I stretch my arms through the sleeves of her jackets, something happens. I become—at once succumbing and resisting, landing in the space between.

系統 (xì tǒng)

System, organization.

Just as I have stopped buying clothes and have been pulling my mother's old clothes over my head, she is pulling me into the folds of her collection. We spend time in the storage room, along with her assistant, where we open box upon box of embroidery. I am creating a filing system for these boxes—a 系統 that organizes the years of my mother's collecting. It's like I am coming up with a weaving notation for her textiles. It is tedious work, work I am doing for my mother because I think it will make her happy. Until I remember to look at the contents of the boxes and find tiny hats and shoes in the shapes of animals—and when I recall what it feels like for me when I am stitching—I imagine the amount of patience and creativity and love it takes for a young woman to stitch just one of these items, and I feel something inside unlock and soften.

繕 (shàn)

Thread + kindness = to mend.

My mother once asked me, "Do you think I'm an artist?"

"You're a collector," was my answer because I didn't want to say no. Or I wasn't sure collectors could be considered artists; even though she has impeccable taste and a discerning eye, I wasn't sure curation could be considered generative creativity. I recoil when my mother suggests I focus my writing on her collection. In my forties, I still have the knee-jerk resistance to the idea that my mother knows what is good for me, even after experience has proven that, for the most part, she does. I have a list of essays I am waiting to write. Most of these topics orbit around motherhood, homecoming, language, and memory. And yet, when I sit down to write, this is what unspools.

What I keep forgetting is that this world of textiles was not one my mother had chosen for herself, either. I am looking for the relationship between text and textile. I want to write in the intricacies of women's work, the dovetailing of thread, the quiet meditative work—and it is work—that slowly, through persistence, becomes art. I want to translate the tactility of textile into language. The language of textile. The title of that essay would be "Why I Stopped Resisting My Mother's Knowledge."

Home

網

It was my father who said that because Billy and I are from such different cultures—white American and Taiwanese—and from such different places—San Diego and Taipei—we shouldn't settle down in either of those places, advising us instead to find a third, neutral location so that it belonged to both of us in equal measure, so that we would begin our life together on the same footing. It wasn't because he didn't wish I could come home to Taiwan—what parent wouldn't want their children to return?—especially since my brother had already married and settled down in Hong Kong and had no inclination of ever moving back to Taiwan. Maybe it was because he already knew his son would not return that he didn't want to allow himself to wish for my return. And so, he told me that it would be better, that it would be easier, to stay away.

∞

My mother and I were invited back to a small room where surgeons rested, read the newspaper, took their lunch. There was a refrigerator so old, when a doctor in a lab coat opened it to store her lunch inside, I noticed that one of the shelves on the door was being held in place with medical tape. Near the refrigerator, mounted next to a wall clock, were two screens. Something flashed onto the screens, adjusting itself up and down. It was a picture of my father's heart. Even though this was a familiar image to her—my father having had bypass surgery and multiple heart procedures—my mother reached out to hold my arm, steadying herself.

This was the first time I had been invited to the viewing room. I had not been in Taiwan during my father's previous surgeries. Today's angiogram—essentially an imaging system using contrast dyes to make arteries in the heart more visible—was being supervised by a close family friend, Dr. Chiu, also in his seventies like my parents. Under his lab coat, he wore a brown flannel shirt tucked into pants hiked way up. He pointed to a thin piece of wire that was searching around my father's chest area, in and around his ribs, playing hide-and-seek. Faintly, I could see the shape of my father's heart—layers of soft grays, like a watered-down Chinese calligraphy painting—as it tightened in two short squeezes.

In the doctor's lounge/surgery viewing room, I watched my father's heart on a computer screen. The second hand on the clock next to it ticked reliably. The tool used to release the contrast dye now looked like a rusty wire hook, and I worried it would accidentally puncture my father's jellyfish heart. At that moment, I had a strange desire to paint the shadows and lights of his ribs, the chambers of this organ that persisted through poor eating habits and hereditary disadvantage. My grandfather had died of a heart attack when he was only forty, a fact my parents brought up often. In his forties, my father was diagnosed with adult-onset diabetes, and my mother, prone to worry and hypochondria, reminded us repeatedly of his conditions.

Suddenly, there were little bursts of darker color, clouds of silky smoke blooming into space. My mother dug her nails into my arm. Were these clouds of blood? Was it perverse that a part of me found what I saw before me arrestingly beautiful? Dr. Chiu explained that this was just the release of contrast dye, which would reveal where the blockages were in my father's heart, where the dangers and threats lurked. He pointed to the parts where my father had his double bypass almost twenty years ago, where medical grade steel twisted, holding tender bits together like the twist ties for bakery bread. Then the dye dissipated, feathered out.

The entire procedure took less than thirty minutes, with Dr. Chiu coming in regularly to update us and explain what was happening—while the angiogram was being taken, the doctors had decided to proceed with an angioplasty, which involves passing balloons through the places where my father's arteries were blocked. Three balloons had squeezed through my father's arteries and popped. The fourth balloon was able to stretch the artery just enough so that the surgeon could insert one stent, bringing the total number of stents in my father's heart to six. Stents are made of a fine wire knitted into a mesh tube and placed strategically where coronary arteries are thickened with plaque, creating space for blood to flow through. How appropriate that the stents inserted into my father's heart worked like knitwear, which has give and pliability, expanding when necessary.

∞

We lived for two years in Singapore and moved to Hong Kong to be closer to family—my brother and a few cousins. In strange ways, Hong Kong made me feel even more foreign than when we were in Singapore. There, we socialized in expat circles with American and Australian lawyers from Billy's work and with retired flight attendants and trailing spouses I met through baby groups. In Hong Kong, in the early 2000s, there was a big influx of affluent businesspeople and families from China, and the government was pushing hard for people to speak Mandarin rather than Cantonese. This was beneficial to me because I didn't speak Cantonese, but it was also clear to me that taxi drivers and the aunties and uncles who sold me fruits and vegetables at the traditional markets and noodle stalls didn't appreciate my not being able to communicate in their language.

In Singapore, I was a new mother. I was trying to write another book. Everything was new and fresh, and even though my writing was muddy, I could forgive myself because I was still green at these new roles. By the time we moved to Hong Kong, our son was almost two years old. I was no longer a new mother; I had no more excuses. But when we applied for our Hong Kong resident cards, I hesitated before filling in "Writer" in the space next to occupation. Our baby was snug in the baby carrier on my chest; I curled my hands around his naked feet for warmth.

Instead, I wrote, "Mother."

∞

By Taiwanese standards, my father is a large man. He has thick, muscular limbs from years of playing competitive rugby and a large, taut belly from his love of food. Perhaps because he is hard of hearing, my father also commands a booming presence in the aural landscape, often startling those around him. My father has always believed that more is more—not in the number of things amassed but in the form of opportunities, friends, experiences, meals. As an entrepreneur, he was constantly looking for the next new thing and considering how to scale ideas into businesses, how to multiply one into many. Besides his main business of children's clothing, he has always maintained a conveyor belt of side businesses: toys, soft-serve ice cream machines, mail-order ascots, a car-service garage, donuts, a haircutting salon for children, even importing large appliances like refrigerators from the US. None of these businesses survived, but failure never made my father's spirit soggy with disappointment. He is a grandiose storyteller, embellishing and conjuring details as he holds court, his listeners rapt with attention. My mother and I would often shoot each other looks when we knew he was stretching truths—it was never in a malicious way, so we allowed his retellings to mushroom into parables. He did sometimes tell jokes at our expense, delivering us—especially my mother—as the punch line. (My father was such a mesmerizing storyteller that it wasn't until recently that I've begun to wonder what my mother's role was in the bravado and flair of all this risk-taking. It is impossible that these stories of loss and redemption belong only to him. Another example of my father's larger-than-life-ness and parallel erasure of my mother's presence: There is a well-known photograph in our family archives of me and my mother walking down a tree-lined street in California. I am two, wearing a navy blue, traditional Chinese quilted robe; my mother is wearing a red jacket and large Austin Powers sunglasses. When my father recalls this photograph, he often inserts himself into the picture as the parent holding my hand.)

People describe my father as a man with a vision and a big heart. Without the stents, his heart would certainly burst. When my mother started to grow into her body in middle age, she showed me how she extended the back clasps of her bra and let out the stitching on the waistbands of her pants and skirts to make space. In a similar way, the stents would act as alterations to accommodate my father's changing body.

∞

I don't think I spent any more time alone in Hong Kong than in Singapore—in fact, we spent weekends with family when our now toddler could play with his cousins—but I became lonely in Hong Kong. Billy was working long hours and traveling. I was able to find a writing group and continued to write, but I have no recollection of what I was actually writing. We wanted more children, but I couldn't get pregnant. Hong Kong felt like an unhappy place, with pressures from China and from the West suffocating local culture and elbowing their way into the already limited physical spaces on the islands. We contributed to that phenomenon.

A friend recommended a holistic-healing center in an office building in Central Hong Kong, where I started to see a doctor, who was an Italian Australian woman, practicing traditional Chinese medicine. She stuck wispy needles into my feet, my shins, my abdomen, my hands, and my forehead and sent me home with Chinese herbs that had been ground into powders the color of incense. I became pregnant with another boy and, not long after that, a girl.

It was time to go home.

∞

Neither my brother nor I grew up with overt pressure to take on the family business. Both of us carved our own paths—my brother was a financial wunderkind, while I, after publishing my first book, continued with Billy's support to write, plodding along slowly but with stubborn determination, even as I committed to the demands of motherhood. When I was little, a family friend asked what I wanted to be when I grew up, and I remember replying, "I want to be a regular person," which I am certain disappointed my father. I loved that he was this larger-than-life personality, but I wanted to be quiet and anonymous to offset his volume and demanding presence. I wanted less in order to counterbalance the abundance he craved and created. Ten years ago, my brother and I both became involved in the business in tangential big-picture roles, which then transformed into more detailed everyday-operational roles. My brother officially took my father's place at the helm with the stoic calm of a dutiful firstborn son. We experience all the situation-appropriate tensions—ricocheting between feeling grateful for the things we have inherited and groaning under the burden of its immeasurable weight.

∞

We wanted to leave Hong Kong, and the only place that made sense for us to go was home to Taiwan. But why did it feel like such a difficult decision? Was my father's advice/warning nagging, like a clothing tag itching and scratching and reminding you of its small existence? What if moving home to Taiwan tipped the balance of our growing family?

∞

Dr. Chiu gently nudged us toward the surgery room, telling us we could go in now to see my father. My mother pushed me ahead. "Too much blood," she whispered.

"Tata!" Dr. Chiu called my father by his childhood nickname. "You're all done!" I followed after, avoiding the blood-soaked, mint-green hospital sheets around my father's chest area. I touched my father's forehead gently, smoothing his head, sparse with hair as it has been for as long as I can remember. His gaze remained toward the ceiling. I remember this exact look, in the post-op room after his bypass several years before. There hadn't been immediate relief, as I thought there would be, but a setting in of fear and vulnerability, a reckoning with mortality.

Standing next to my father's gurney now, his eyes unblinking, I wanted something—a noise, a joke, a distraction—to jolt him back to life, back to his usual self. I helped the nurse push him back to hospital room 714, where he had left his phone, charger, a book on Taoism, and his reading glasses on the bedside table. On top of the little refrigerator in the corner of the room, my mother had already gathered Tupperwares of freshly cut fruit, bottles of water, and brewed tea.

Convalescence proceeded quickly with childhood friends visiting, bringing boxes of peaches and guava. They crowded into the small room, sitting wherever they could find a space, and reminisced about the past, sharing their latest ailments and laughing about growing old together. Dr. Chiu came first thing each morning, as well as other doctor friends of varying—and completely unrelated—specialties who happened to be in the hospital. Ever the extrovert, my father's deflated sense of vulnerability quickly dissipated, buoyed by the energy and constant company of other people. Within two days, my father, with a new passageway opened up in his heart, was discharged. He was giddy and confident he wouldn't be returning any time soon.

∞

We packed our bags and moved to Taiwan. For the first few months, we lived with my parents in the apartment where I had grown up. Billy was still with the same job, so he commuted to and from Hong Kong and was absent for the better part of the week. Billy was frustrated at having to spend so much time away from us, and when he was in Taipei, he didn't like having to wake up in my parents' house, not being able to be in our own space. He had visited Taiwan numerous times before we were married; he even spent a summer interning at a law firm. He loved Taiwan then, but the current circumstances made his experience of our move disjointed. On one of his weekends after being away, we decided to go out to dinner, just the two of us, after we'd put the kids to bed, and on the cab ride, he expressed irritation at the inconvenience of the banking system in Taiwan, followed by a comment on how unfriendly the user interface of many websites could be—for example, when we were looking for someplace to eat that evening, there wasn't an easy way to figure out, with information in English, what places were around my parents' neighborhood; finally, he ended by saying, "Taiwanese food isn't even that good." I looked out the window, afraid to talk or meet his gaze, because if I did, I would start crying.

During the week while he was away, I hauled the children around town, reacquainting myself with Taiwan, and I felt myself falling madly in love. Every experience we had—whether at the local 7-Eleven perusing snacks from my childhood, like Yakult and tea eggs, shopping for produce at the wet market and chatting with the uncles and aunties who were always ready with a sample for the kids and a recipe idea for me to try, or stopping off at the many playgrounds that dotted the city, with slides and swings and exercise equipment for the elderly—was like a delightful confirmation that I did, in fact, love Taiwan. And I loved it differently, now that I had children. I already knew that I wanted this to be the place we would stay and settle in. I also knew that Billy wasn't convinced yet and that I couldn't push or rush him. My conviction that we had found home felt like an affair I had to keep secret.

Our children were six, three, and eighteen months and needed constant care and attention. I remember my mother telling me how different her father was as a grandfather. He had been a stern parent—opinionated, respected, distant. When I was born, before we moved into a house, my mother lived in a small apartment in South San Francisco with her parents, my three-year-old brother, and her younger sister while my father was in Taiwan. In the middle of the night, when I cried for milk, it was my grandfather who got up quietly to go to the kitchen to warm the water on the stove to mix with formula; it was my grandfather who would bring the bottle to my mother, who was stunned by this gesture of care. I witnessed the same transformation with my own father too, but even more dramatically.

When my brother and I were growing up, our father's presence was not consistent and his love was general. He was broadly supportive of our endeavors, but when he was not busy with work, he preferred to spend his time with friends, dreaming up business ideas on the golf course, discussing politics across smoky mah-jong tables. But when my children were born, my father became fascinated with their every expression and honest response to the world. The attention he had for my young children was focused and whole. He was so eager to please them, so desperate for them to love him, it irritated me. I watched the way he played with my children—flinging them up in the air, dancing and singing with them, offering them treats behind my back—and felt my heart pucker and wrinkle with jealousy.

Billy told me I should only feel happy that someone besides the two of us loved our children so fiercely. Isn't this the reason we moved to Taiwan?

∞

And then, just a week after the angioplasty, while at a friend's house playing mah-jong, my father felt a cold sweat as his stomach twisted into knots. He left the game, hurrying into a taxi. When the mah-jong host had realized a fourth player had gone missing, she quickly called my mother, who was home at the time, and waited for my father anxiously at the mouth of their alley. When he arrived, she found him keeled over in pain, his forehead hot with fever. They rushed to the emergency room.

He remained feverish for two days. His doctor friends—the cardiologist, the urologist, even the head of ENT—made the rounds, each with his own diagnosis. The one thing they all agreed on was that my father was to be kept in the hospital for a full week of observations. They printed out an impromptu sign that read, "No visitors, please," and taped it to his door. This time, he was in room 618. It's astounding how quickly you get used to life at the hospital—you know where to get ice, heating pads, extra blankets. You become familiar with the on-duty nurses, at first wondering about their own families, their lives outside of the hospital, but quickly becoming dependent on their devotion to the patients and patience with the family. Because the doctors had ruled out any gastrointestinal issues, my father was allowed to refuse hospital food, which, to him, was a small triumph. My mother found a Japanese place nearby where we got takeout multiple times, a neighborhood coffee shop with a strong brew for our morning and afternoon coffees.

The fever had nothing to do with his recent heart procedure. Turned out, it was a urinary tract infection due to an enlarged prostate. It wasn't as dire as we had feared, but it added to the growing list of health issues that needed attention. My father used to play golf five days a week before heading into the office, where he ran his company all day; he went out to business and social dinners and traveled at least twice a month. Now, because of a bad knee and a recent shoulder surgery, he could play golf only once a month, and with a different set of friends, who average higher scores, shorter distances, and more lenient handicaps. He was fitted for a hearing aid recently. He had been advised by his doctor to walk with a cane after taking several falls. He was due for cataract surgery soon.

∞

One weekend when Billy was in Taipei, we brought the kids to the beach. He had grown up next to the ocean and often felt its tidal pull, especially when things were stirred up or unmoored. A swim in the ocean always helped clear his mind. Before we started our summer program in Russia, our study group convened in Finland—officially, where we first met—and we stayed in a simple business hotel on the gulf. At the orientation, I remember noticing him across the conference room. I don't know how we were introduced, but we exchanged names, and one of the first things he said to me was that I looked younger than twenty. And then he said he was going to go out back behind the hotel and see if he could figure out a way to swim in the gulf. His need to plunge himself in a natural body of water made an impression on me. I, too, had grown up surrounded by the ocean, yet my relationship to it, like that of many Taiwanese people, was always one of fear fueled by two notions—one, that the tides would swallow you and two, that China would swallow you.

Perhaps for those reasons, the beach was only sparsely populated on the day we went. It was a windy day. As soon as we were on the beach and the children could be unfurled from our arms, they scattered, running away from us toward the water and then back to us again, their wispy hair in their faces and in their open, laughing mouths, then out again toward the water they would go. Billy had taken each of the children into the ocean when they were just four or five months old, holding them and dipping them into and under the water. All three of them were startled by their first underwater experience, but all three emerged from the ocean safe in their father's arms, leaning against his tanned, freckled shoulder. This was before any of them had eaten seasoned food, and I remember how much they liked to slurp on their sea salt fingers.

We walked behind our children, who zigzagged away from and toward us, each time widening the distance between. An elderly couple was walking along the beach, the wife holding a parasol that kept threatening to flip inside out in the wind. The husband studied our configuration, likely calculating our relationship. He looked at me, nodded three times at the screeching kids, then looked back at me and asked, his voice loud and filled with velocity, "All of these yours?" I nodded. Clearly surprised and very impressed, he stopped and clapped his hands together and bowed his head.

"The country thanks you for your contribution." The old man was referring to the dismal and ever-declining birth rate in Taiwan. Billy and I looked at each other and smiled.

The day before we were about to sign the lease for an apartment near the schools the children would be attending—our oldest at the K–12 international school I had attended and the younger two at a little Montessori nursery near the river, walking distance from the apartment—my mother called and said a friend of hers had heard about a house that was available. The only time I had ever lived in a house was when we lived in San Francisco during the first four years of my life. All my memories of living in that house are of floor-level textures—the carpet, the refrigerator door, the coffee table, the leaves in the yard, the rough, skid-free tiles in the changing room at the public pool we would go to with my cousins. I don't recall the spatial hollowness of living in our own house, but, after we had moved to Taiwan and lived exclusively in apartments, I remember visiting my cousins in the summers and never knowing where people were. They could be upstairs, downstairs, in corners and under stairs, or worse, out in the yard or in the garage. It felt difficult to keep track, whereas, in the apartments of my youth, we could easily hear where people were and, generally, what they were doing. I knew when my mother was awake because I would hear the rustle of plastic bags in the kitchen as she unwrapped fruits and vegetables from the wet market; I knew when my father was in a good mood because I could hear him blasting Italian opera on his stereo. When my father used to drink at dinner parties and had overindulged, my brother and I could clearly hear him retch in his bathroom. The sounds in the apartment kept us close, even if we didn't necessarily address each other's needs.

Of course, Billy had only ever lived in houses in California; really, one main one where he could walk to and from school, to and from the beach. We were married five minutes from his childhood home, which was sold after his father passed away; for years afterward, he would dream of that house. There have been so many mornings when, the two of us still lying in bed, he would recount a dream where he was inside the house, needing to protect it somehow, trying—often in vain—to lock the doors, that I have come to know the interiors of that home as though it's a space I have inhabited, even though I have only driven by and looked at its exterior. But I can feel the rootedness that this house—and perhaps houses in general—provided for Billy. Houses represent key facets of the American spirit—the ability to build, to own, to be independent.

When we walked into the house that was for rent, we could see into a yard and into our neighbors' yards on both sides. In the distance, the layered mountains looked like an ink painting. School was just a fifteen-minute walk down the hill. We were a thirty-minute car ride away from my parents' apartment. As Billy looked out the window, I felt him soften and knew we had just changed the architecture of what home would look like for us in Taiwan.

∞

One afternoon, my father looked at me from the hospital bed and touched my arm imploringly.

He asked, "Is this the moment I get old?"

Since retirement, my father has been fulfilling his lifelong dream of wearing his hair long. He used to let my mother dress him in clothes that she would design and make specially for his atypically large frame—she bought raw silks from Thailand, linens from western China, indigo from the mountains in Taiwan, and crafted them into shirts with mandarin collars and sleeves that went to my father's elbow. That had become my father's signature look, a complement to my mother's even more refined style, the nuances of which I appreciate more the older I get. But now, like a man loosening his tie after a long day's work, my father has taken to wearing large T-shirts, shorts, and sandals, looking every bit like the seventies' hippie he'd once aspired to emulate during his brief time living in the US, in Fresno, California, of all places, trying the States on to see whether he would ultimately immigrate, as the rest of his family had done, as his then-girlfriend, my mother, was also ready to do. In the end, my father convinced my mother to return to Taiwan, and here they were now—my father lying in the hospital bed, his shoulder-length gray hair undone from its ponytail so that he could lie flat on his pillow, stray wisps of hair in his face, the rest of it spread out on the pillow in a knotted mass, his beard white and untamed after just a week in the hospital.

"I think," my father continued, "growing old happens in an instant." He rolled more squarely onto his back and stared up at the ceiling. "Is this the moment for me?"

Part of the charisma that attracts people to my father is his unapologetic honesty. At times this has made social situations uncomfortable, especially if the topic is politically charged, but ultimately, people admire his no-holds-barred style, especially in a culture where meaning is most often extracted from what is not said, from the negative spaces between and underneath sentences. Plus it makes him fun to be around—without him, meals are just meals, but with him at the table, it becomes a party. My father has never been shy about the litany of failed businesses he has poured money into over the years. Being immersed in the family business now, I am discovering just how complex building and running a business can be and how helping out is not always straightforward—or even helpful, really. I am learning it is possible to inherit the negative spaces too. The untold stories, the ones that fizzle out or disappoint.

∞

Once we moved into the house, something opened up for us. We had distance from my parents and from my childhood home. Together, we could design and structure our life in Taiwan in our own way and with new coordinates. Billy decided to leave his current job so that he didn't have to commute on an airplane each week and could actually be in Taiwan. At the same time, I started helping out with the family business, going into the office a few days a week, having lunch with my parents without the distraction of my children.

And, when we brought the children to see my parents on the occasional weekend, I could allow that the way my father loved and doted on my children was, as Billy had suggested, a good thing.

∞

"You're not old," I told my father.

At first, I was bewildered by his question—his not knowing he was old.

But I think he was trying to say—it's not that one grows old in an instant; it's that one's recognition of it happens in an instant. I realized that his moment of recognition ran parallel with one of my own—of being counted on as the adult in the room. The elbow my mother reached for to steady herself. The one to push my father's gurney. At his shoulder surgery some months before, I was the one who filled out hospital forms for him. Even when I first became a mother more than a decade ago, I didn't immediately feel grown up. Strangers would respond with genuine surprise when they found out I had a child, but as the child became two children, and the two became three, I gradually morphed into the part I was playing. One day, a café barista addressed me as "ma'am," and that was that. Still, that others had begun to recognize me as the adult in the room didn't mean I identified as a grown-up myself.

In a letter to the daughter she never had, Maya Angelou writes, "I am convinced that most people do not grow up. We find parking spaces and honor our credit cards. We marry and dare to have children and call that growing up. I think what we do is mostly grow old. We carry accumulation of years in our bodies and on our faces, but generally our real selves, the children inside, are still innocent and shy as magnolias."

I'm still not quite sure whether I agree with Maya Angelou that we don't grow up and only grow old. But I do think she's right that, at our core, we are still innocent young children. In my case, I can easily recall the same shyness, timidity, and contemplative wonder with which I regarded the world when I was nine years old. I can still call up the same quiet desire—"shy as magnolias"—for my parents to see me as I really am.

Other signs of my father's aging (much more pronounced than the long list of physical ailments): He has taken up Chinese calligraphy and writes page after page of poetry, lines of philosophy. After handing over his business to my brother, he has begun to talk about the beauty of smallness, suggesting that not everything has to be scalable. Enough can be enough. This, too, makes my heart prickle. Does growing old allow you to pass something down while changing the rules? But this pivot also gives me tremendous relief. He is giving us permission to scale down, only make what is necessary, be quiet.

It's strange to watch a large person retreat, disquieting to notice the whispers tucked between the pronouncements. Toward the end of his hospital stay, when he felt he could get out of bed, I wheeled my father down to the hospital's hair salon to get his hair washed. While shampooing his hair—Taiwanese hairdressers can perform this task expertly while the person sits upright in the barber chair—the hairdresser studied my father's scalp and observed that he was sprouting new hairs. My father's eyes lit up. "Really?"

"Of course!" she said, pulling up a few strands of short, sudsy hair from the top of my father's head. "It must be because you have less stress," she looked in my direction, "now that you are being taken care of." I was sitting in the barber chair next to my dad, and he smiled at me in the mirror.

Maybe there is a sliver of time when we become grown-ups, but it doesn't have to do with jobs and responsibilities or caretaking, whether of growing children or aging parents, which is accelerated by returning home as an adult. Maybe becoming a grown-up occurs the moment we see our parents as they really are, a moment of forgiveness.

In reexamining my dad's stories—his self-aggrandizement and parallel diminishing of my mother—I should also reconsider the stories my mother told. When my parents refer to the four to five years they spent apart, with my father in Taiwan and my mother in the United States, the emphasis is always on my mother's capability and the courage it took for her to care for two young children on her own in a foreign country while her husband tested out his entrepreneurial ideas in Taiwan. I still marvel at her hardiness, especially now after having gone through that intense, physically taxing, and lonely period of parenting young toddlers. But in celebrating and honoring my mother's fortitude, have I minimized my father's loneliness during that same period? I think of all the times I called home the twenty years I spent away from Taiwan—from college onward—and how, whenever my father picked up the telephone, I would immediately bypass him and ask for my mother.

Recently, I noticed that my father's eyes were unusually swollen and glassy. He admitted his vision was blurring, and I wondered out loud whether it was still possible for him to write calligraphy. He snorted, as if he were about to call me stupid, the way he easily chided us when we were young, but he caught himself and instead said, "You don't write calligraphy with your eyes. You write it with your heart."

On Women's Work and Creativity

繡, 織, 編

The history of clothing and textiles can be dated as far back as 100,000 to 500,000 years ago. It's difficult to arrive at a more precise time period, because textiles are notoriously vulnerable to the environment, as they naturally disintegrate over time. But we do know that weaving and, later, knitting, sewing, and embroidery were all relegated to "women's work" across cultures. This was the case, in large part, because childminding was a woman's main role in the family, and her additional contributions had to be work that she could perform while simultaneously taking care of children—in other words, work that was repetitive, didn't require too much focused attention, and she could easily return to it amidst constant interruption.

∞

I wasn't working when my first baby was born, but I harbored wild fantasies of writing a book—multiple books!—during this time. When I read Rachel Cusk's *A Life's Work,* I marveled at the feat of a woman writing about the mutual exclusivity of new motherhood and creativity and yet still writing through that wall, the proof of which was in my hands. I furiously underlined sentences about loneliness and frustration, corroborated with exclamation points in the margins. I tried to emulate Cusk and created a folder on my computer titled, "Notes on Motherhood." I already had a folder titled "Notes on Pregnancy," which I dutifully contributed to for thirty-six weeks, until the baby's early arrival; his first interruption. The new folder was sparsely populated with flimsy threads of notes. I think I was grateful to have a place to go to when I was free from childminding. But when my baby cried, I wilted and lost all resolve to do anything but go to him, scoop him from his helplessness, and press him against my chest and sway and shush and offer my breast.

New motherhood was a portal into a parallel existence where time was spliced into tiny segments, each segment marked by interruption that was physical, urgent, a matter of life. I couldn't *not* be pulled away. These interruptions were not of my own doing. I could not be blamed for my fraying focus. I was being called toward something necessary and real, a need only I could fulfill physically.

"Notes on Motherhood" remained mostly empty, and what I did put down in writing was diaphanous, like gauzy curtains fluttering in the wind. But what I remember of my thinking and discoveries and figuring during that time is that it was all complex and intertwined and important. I was acquiring—or was I being reintroduced to?—a kind of embodied knowledge that didn't have a language I could yet speak. The structures of logic in my mind were helixed and knotted and webbed, and my mind seemed to contract and expand like my baby's belly, which I watched, mesmerized by his breathing, while he slept. What I was beginning to understand about my place in the world could not be translated into words. Not yet at least. But I was desperate to try.

∞

In *Women's Work: The First 20,000 Years*, Elizabeth Wayland Barber, writing about the study of textiles, says that, because they are "perishable, the textiles themselves are not easy to learn about—just like most of the rest of women's products (such as food and the recipes for preparing it)." Unlike iron or brass weapons, concrete buildings, or large ships that were built by men with materials that are solid, heavy, and tangible, and that remain largely intact through time, what women's work produces frays and unravels. But women's work is just as—if not more—essential to our survival inside and outside the home. Women's work is the thread that secures the stone mallet to its handle, the tarp that shelters and protects, the woven sail that helps propel large ships on voyages. These fine threads are the connective tissues that hold us together and keep us warm, the threads that tether us to home and unravel to let us go, leaving a tail so that we can always find our way back.

∞

I spent the first year of motherhood either ensconced in the midday quiet of being at home with the baby or blindly feeling my way in the dark from my room down the hall to the baby's room. The aural landscape of those days had a muffled hollowness, like being submerged underwater or cloistered in a small space, such as a phone booth with the door closed but with no one on the other end of the line. Few words were spoken, and what was communicated was mainly expressed through touch. Touch, but also the invisible thread that, because it was only recently cut, still connected us through vibrational signals. Scientifically, the calls of my baby, which I felt bodily—from the next room, from the kitchen—could probably be explained as hormones, but it felt even more real than science; it was more like faith, simultaneously inexplicable and grounded. As a father, Billy was devoted and attentive and patient and already fun, but he was a wake-time father. He never stirred in the middle of the night, not because he was ignoring the baby's cries, but because he physically could not hear or feel the baby's pleas. I often leapt out of bed before the baby started whimpering. Of course, the signal was often a breast pad that had been soaked through with milk, but it was also just as often a tugging that I could feel in my lower abdomen, where the baby was once nestled.

How many times did I feel my way in the dark, palms against the cool walls, toes gripping the wooden floors, eyes barely opened, my consciousness slipping between sleep and wakefulness in a plane where my baby and I met? I breathed in the scent of his urgent need to be held, enveloping his little body in my arms, swallowing his cries. When I could feel his energy wanting to fizz up into wakefulness, I swayed in the dark and hummed the lullaby my mother sang to me, slowly, softly, barely audible. I stretched each note as long as I could and breathed in a lungful of air after two notes. I would often become lightheaded, but exhaling these notes always guaranteed my baby's body would become heavy with sleep.

Women's work is the collection of the little things we do in the dark—nursing, whispering lullabies, rubbing backs, placing the backs of our hands on warm foreheads, dropping water onto the insides of our wrists to test its temperature—quiet, tactile gestures that remind us how much of human survival depends upon the warmth of these basic, small physical connections.

And yet, tactile memory feels like it is the easiest to lose.

∞

The majority of children's textiles in my mother's collection come from the Miao, who teach their girls the techniques of cloth making, weaving, dyeing, and embroidery from the age of four. Women's work, in Miao culture, is not something that is *relegated* to women; it is *endowed* and *entrusted* to women. Inheriting the practice of cloth making and cloth decorating is a source of pride; it is also a practice that is paramount to the recording of Miao history. The poetic irony for this culture, which doesn't have a written language in the sense that Western education understands it, is that "illiteracy" and not attending school has helped preserve the art of writing and recording through the techniques of embroidery. Embroidery in Miao culture is referred to as 女書, "female script." Along with a rich oral tradition, weaving and embroidery are the mediums through which histories, origin stories, and observations of the natural and spiritual world are depicted and passed down to the next generation. In Miao culture, women weave the fabric of collective memory.

Women's work produces female script, an encoded language that is not the kind of language we automatically think of under Western education, which is usually written or spoken. Female script is composed of nouns that are motifs and verbs that are textures and adjectives that are colors and tones that are patterns.

∞

But even as, in new motherhood, I was relearning the language of tactility and feeling my way into a knowingness that transcended language, language—Mandarin, which I wanted to pass down to my children, and English, which is the language I write in—insisted itself into my brain. It was instinctual for me to try to translate my first experiences of motherhood into words because words are my medium. The realization that words—in either language of my upbringing—were inadequate frustrated me and, at the same time, pushed me to try harder. *Essai* in French, the origin of the English word *essay,* means "to try, to attempt." If textile represented women's work and motherhood, then I was trying to look for the text in textile.

∞

Evidence suggests that, as early as the Neolithic era—about 4000 BCE—women began to spend extra time on cloth making, adding designs and embellishments so that what they produced transcended mere function. As such, "along with cave paintings, threads were among the earliest transmitters of meaning," writes Anni Albers in her book *On Weaving.* Like language, textile can relay information—the specific colors, techniques, and symbols adorning textiles can denote social rank, record history, and narrate folktales, all the while acting as a kind of protective covering. Elizabeth Wayland Barber writes in *Women's Work,* "Ethnographic parallels worldwide show that enormous time is often put into 'simply' decorating people and things with efficacious symbols believed to promote life, prosperity, and safety. . . . Thus 'art' is at once pleasing and thoroughly functional—a double winner." And yet, perhaps because of the practicality of textiles—such as clothing, bedding, floor and wall coverings—even if highly decorative, they were rarely considered art. Furthermore, perhaps because the technical skills involved—weaving, sewing, and embroidery—were skills all girls were once expected to learn, the quotidian nature of these skills downgraded what they produced into necessities and, at best, crafts.

When we consider what makes something art, a sense of uselessness is typically associated with it—the idea of art for art's sake. Of course, art has a real function in defining culture, in being a necessary medium through which human emotions and the human condition during a certain time are translated, but the things we use in everyday life are rarely considered art. Art has traditionally belonged in another realm—one that sits above the practical; its being use*less* is often cited as the very reason for its cultural significance and superiority. However, as Albers so astutely writes, "Usefulness does not prevent a thing, anything, from being art. We must conclude, then, that it is the thoughtfulness and care and sensitivity in regard to form that makes a house turn into art, and that it is this degree of thoughtfulness, care, and sensitivity that we should try to attain."

In other words, to be a creative person, to be an artist requires, first and foremost, a practice of sustained and whole attention, a kind of "thoughtfulness, care, and sensitivity" I began to embody in motherhood.

∞

I have an odd memory I return to often when I think of the invisible work of motherhood. I am maybe ten or eleven, and while taking a shower one day, I notice that the bottom third of the shower curtain is dotted with fuzzy specks of gray mildew in various sizes. Next to where I am showering, a small window opens into the alleyway between our apartment building and the construction going on next door. A whoosh of alley wind blows into the bathroom and, on its way out the window again, slaps the shower curtain onto my bare legs. I shudder in disgust, peeling the flimsy nylon away from my body. I make a note to tell my mother about the moldy shower curtain but inevitably forget. The next day, when I prepare to take a shower after dinner, I notice that the curtain is brand new—dazzling white and made of a thicker, sturdier material. I ask my mother about it, and she replies, nonchalantly, that she had noticed the old one had started sprouting mold and went out and got a new curtain that day. Then she reminds me to untuck the curtain from the inside rim of the bathtub after my shower so it can dry more thoroughly and prevent mold from growing.

My mother did countless tasks for us each day to keep us fed, clothed, and safe, but the new shower curtain was the first time the invisibility of her work materialized for me. She was not the kind of mother who made things with her hands. Like her own mother, mine worked outside the home, so she wasn't a kitchen mom or a mom who was constantly hanging up clothes to dry on the balcony. And though the results of her "women's work" were not traditional handmade textiles—even if the subject of her study and collection would later become that—what I learned that day was that women's work is not just about spinning threads and mending holes; in a broader sense, women's work is care through sustained attention. So much of caretaking is about tending to loved ones with thoughtful attention. If we apply Alber's view of art as, in part, the result of sensitivity and thoughtfulness, then it is possible to see caretaking—the most primal form of which is motherhood—as an expression of creativity. A mother's first act of creativity: bringing life into the world.

But we don't go about our days thinking about this poetic exaltation of motherhood. Instead, like the cheap nylon shower curtain splattered with mold, the work of caretaking can often feel flimsy, insignificant, and unbeautiful. Caring for my babies required tending to an endless sequence of bodily functions—nursing, wiping, burping, changing soiled diapers, bathing, dozing. If pregnancy welcomed me back into my physical self, then childminding surrendered me to the baby's physical needs, heightening my sensitivity to the connective tissues that simultaneously cleaved us together and would eventually cleave us from one another.

> Contronyms are words that have two meanings, which are opposite of each other. *Cleave* can mean "to bind together" or "to cut apart." Another contronym: *Ravel* can mean "to separate," as in threads in cloth, or "to entangle."

And isn't that the basis of motherhood—or, perhaps, of our collective existence—the simultaneity of holding on and letting go, of the accumulation of useless tasks in the hopes of creating some larger meaning? And if, in our lifetime, we are able to render some facet of understanding of being, then what? I would like to imagine that this is my women's work, that I am laying down the threads for my children to find their way home in the distant future, after they have cleaved themselves from me, after they have returned all their tactile memories of being held in my arms to me, after I have watched their shrinking backs yet again, hoping that this time they might turn around and come home.

∞

What are the threads that I am laying down for my children so that they can find their way home one day?

Nationality

絡

Taichung, 1958

For a week, she stood inside a room at the Taichung train station. There was something quietly defiant about her stance, left foot crossed over her right, the weight of her body slightly on the back foot, as if she were just about to take a small step forward. Her chin was tilted up so that her eyes, not fully shut, received light, and her eyelids were pearly and diaphanous. She held a soft gaze, not focusing on anything in particular but able to take in everything.

Everything else on the inventory list of items that was to be transported by train from the provincial government office in Taipei had been accounted for, picked up, and delivered by truck to the office's new location in Taichung. This move to decentralize government operations was a preventative measure intended to protect against air raids from China. Perhaps someone up north in Taipei had left her off the list so that the movers in Taichung didn't know she belonged with the rest of the valuables and was thus regarded as trash.

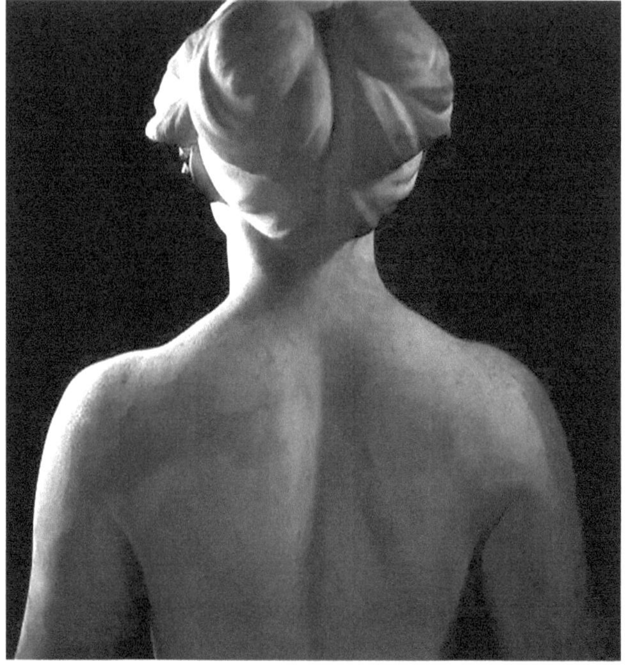

© Huang Pang-Chuan, Lin Chunni

Certainly, her nudity horrified some who saw her—her marble flesh white and supple, the sturdy curvature of her thighs, the intimate crook of her elbow, the slight depression in her left nipple, and the soft roundness of her abdomen, which led to the triangle mound of flesh that had been, in what must have been an act of anger and disgust by a passing vandal, defaced and smeared in ink. The Taichung train station had been built under Japanese occupation in a Baroque style—theatrical and ostentatiously European—and should have served as a fitting backdrop for her, but, unlike the train station, which was a remnant of colonization most could accept, she was modern in the wrong way. She was too exposed. Or could it be that as a witness to the fracture in the current society—Taiwan had only recently struggled violently to define itself and was now suffering the continued fate of an island being colonized, ceded, and used by larger powers, suppressed and silenced by martial law—her steady gaze exposed too much?

The head of the freight company who had been contracted for this move was alerted to her existence a week after the job had been completed. He called his nephew, a doctor who dabbled in the arts in his off time, telling him that something of interest had been found and to hurry to the train station. When he arrived, the doctor recognized her at once. He was not one to bare his emotions easily, but his eyes filled with hot tears when he saw that she had been treated as garbage and sullied by ink. He had her trucked to his home immediately. He instructed workmen to lay down steel pipes in order to roll her heavy body gently across the floor. She glided effortlessly toward the corner of the doctor's dining room, where she was set down and stood for the next sixteen years.

Her arrival was at first met with excitement by the doctor's six young children, but, as children adapt readily to new things, they quickly accepted her as a part of the family, even referring to her as Jie Jie, "older sister." The children passed her numerous times each day, grazing her cool marble body. When they came home from school, they dropped their school bags next to her feet. Sometimes, the two youngest girls would sit on the floor and hug her legs in easy adoration. When, after dinner, the children dawdled over their schoolwork, their mother would tease that Jie Jie was watching, and if they didn't finish their work, she would be upset.

Whereas the children lived easily with her presence, the doctor experienced a seismic shift. When she first arrived, the oldest son noticed that his father would often take a washcloth to her to wipe away the ink. He toweled her gently and diligently, but the mark could not be erased; the black splatter was now blue, like a bruise. On the weekends, the doctor began inviting artists to his home; he sat with them in the dining room to draw and paint under her encouraging gaze. In his work tending to patients, one of his favorite tasks was setting broken bones with casts; he delighted in the tactile sensation of molding the plaster and using his understanding of the human body to coax fractures toward healing. In addition to painting, he started to sculpt with clay, using his fingers to nudge and shape animal and human forms. He had the children chase after a neighborhood cat and bring it home to model for him. His mother, wife, and daughters also sat for him. As a doctor, he had studied anatomy and learned the intricate ways the inner mechanisms of the body were constantly in motion. A few friends had suggested he sculpt using her as a model; why not learn from the master? No, the doctor was adamant he could never do that.

When he looked at her standing in his dining room—the way her marble skin dappled in the light, how he could see the muscles underneath, the way she tilted her chin up simultaneously in defiance and in surrender—he imagined an artist's continual attempt to depict movement, to embody life. This moved the doctor deeply.

The doctor never spoke directly about her or divulged her true identity, but that she had ignited something in him was a certainty everyone in the family could see.

Tokyo, 1921

The young sculptor from Taiwan was often ridiculed by his classmates at the art school in Tokyo. He was the son of a woodworker, and his name—consisting of the characters for *dirt* and *water*—evoked a crude simplicity in stark contrast to his more affluent, well-clothed peers. He worked diligently, late into the night, so that he had no time for social niceties, yet another strike against his character. But his sculptures—first wood then marble—were exceptional, and curators of the Japanese Imperial Art Exhibition took notice.

It was only after leaving that the distance allowed him to consider the contours of home more thoughtfully. And because he had been transported to the land of the colonizer, questions of identity and culture begged urgent answers. Such was the young sculptor's state of mind when his first piece of art was selected for the Imperial Exhibition, a sculpture of a naked Indigenous Taiwanese boy playing a flute. For the sculptor, his subject was a foray into describing what it might mean to be from Taiwan. For the Japanese art world, the subject was an exotic depiction of life on their "ghost island" colony. Meanwhile, both on the ghost island and in dormitories for Taiwanese students studying in Japan, a passionate movement for self-governance was developing. And because, under Japanese rule, colonized Taiwanese were not allowed to gather for political reasons, the cultural movement was built through the arts—through paintings, sculptures, theater, and poetry.

The sculptor yearned for an artistic style and perspective unique to Taiwan, especially as a departure from Chinese culture, which he viewed as traditional and staid. "It is human nature," he declared, "to love the country you were born in, and to love the land you were born on. Although it is said that art knows no national boundaries, and can be created anywhere, we all ultimately long for the land on which we were born. Our beautiful Taiwan, the Ilha Formosa, conjures even more longing."

The Japanese Imperial Art Exhibition selected a second piece by the twenty-six-year-old sculptor. This time his subject was a young girl, nude, emerging from a clamshell with an expression of confidence and hope on her face.

Her eyes are not quite closed, and in that sliver of opening, she looks simultaneously out at the world and in at the rippling pools of her soul. This is a look often seen in sculptures of Buddha or Guanyin, the goddess of mercy, but their eyes are most often depicted in a downward cast, whereas the sculptor's young girl looks up, as though searching for light. Her physique is solid; seen from behind, the gentle arch of her back brings attention to her upward gaze. One can make a swift connection to Botticelli's *The Birth of Venus,* with its nude Venus rising out of a shell from the sea. In Botticelli's painting, Venus covers her right breast demurely with her hand and uses her long locks to cover her pubic area, whereas the sculptor's young girl stands with both hands resting behind her on the opened clam shell from which she has materialized, unapologetic and honest about her form in its most natural state.

The sculptor worked without rest, hammering a slab of rough and unformed marble bit by bit, coaxing it into soft, smooth flesh. He used his hands to transform the property of matter, used his fingers to feel across the surface of her back, the shadow of indentation below her bottom lip, the knobs of muscle above her knees. His yearning for home, for a sense of Taiwan, for a stance that leaned toward independence was realized in her.

The sculptor called her Gan Lu Shui, or Water of Immortality, a reference to the purest of liquids inside the vial Guanyin often holds between her fingers, as well as a metaphor for the dew from which new life springs forth.

After she was selected for the 1921 Imperial Art Exhibition, the sculptor continued to work until his death just nine years later, becoming one of the most well-regarded sculptors in Taiwan. She traveled home to Taiwan and was displayed in a government building in Taipei.

Gan Lu Shui was last seen by the public when the provincial office was moved to Taichung.

Taichung, 1974

The doctor had fallen gravely ill. He was feverish and always cold and could not find comfort, even when wrapped in heavy blankets. The children were grown now, the eldest performing his conscription services on Kinmen Island. Taiwan was in its twenty-fifth year of martial law. Much of the lived history of Taiwan the doctor had experienced was erased from history textbooks and never taught in school. The atmosphere of fear from the White Terror years lingered like a fog that never lifts, forever clouding one's vision.

The doctor knew he had very little time left. For sixteen years, Gan Lu Shui lived with the family; she watched his children grow up, watched the doctor grow older, and watched him become ill. She was a secret the doctor protected, knowing that one day she would have to be returned to her rightful home, the government of Taiwan. But he had found her at a time when she was cast away as trash by a government in turmoil, and he had never felt it was safe for her to reemerge without risk of castigation, ill-intentioned ownership, or worse—destruction.

She had been a steady presence in the doctor's life, reigniting his passion for art. But he feared that when he was no longer able to care for her, she might become a burden to his family. He made a decision. The doctor wrapped her up in sheets of linen and heavy blankets and sealed her in a wooden box, transporting her to a family-owned factory in Wufeng, an agricultural suburb of Taichung, tucking her under a nondescript staircase. Aside from the doctor's wife and his eldest son, he told no one where she was hidden. He and his wife agreed Gan Lu Shui could only be seen again when Taiwan society recognized its multiple cultures, languages, and histories, when people could really listen to one another with respect. Gan Lu Shui could only be returned to a Taiwan confident in its identity.

The doctor passed away two years after he secreted Gan Lu Shui.

Taipei, 2021

When he was growing up, the doctor's oldest son never learned from his father who she was and only by chance saw a photograph of Jie Jie in an art magazine, along with a caption that said her whereabouts were unclear. He thought it odd, of course, because for sixteen years, she lived right in his family's dining room. But he knew not to delve deeper, understanding that when adults skirted around an issue, spoke in hushed tones, or switched to Japanese so that children couldn't understand what was being said, the topic was off-limits. Schooling in Taiwan in the 1960s and '70s successfully drove a wedge between generations. Not only did fathers and sons speak different languages, textbooks taught sweeping Chinese history, of which Taiwan's history constituted only a few thin pages. It wasn't until the doctor's son left Taiwan to attend medical school in Japan that he truly began to question the heavy silence that burdened his adolescence. Much later, he thought, "You know what brainwashing is? Brainwashing is when you can't speak with your own father."

The doctor's son grew up to be a doctor too, and like his father, he was drawn to the arts. He designed the home he lived in with his wife and two children and would sometimes paint in his spare time. From time to time, people would come around asking about Gan Lu Shui, but the doctor's son kept quiet, wholeheartedly understanding his father's wish to protect her until the right moment. This kind of silence—born from respect and grace—was his father's legacy. She remained in the wooden box underneath a metal staircase in the factory in Wufeng, which made plastic parts for sewing machines and cassette tapes. She stayed there quietly, as machines whirred and fans blew and busy hands worked, for forty-seven years. And the doctor's son also waited quietly for the right moment to arise.

Exactly one century after the young sculptor completed Gan Lu Shui, the moment arrived. The doctor's son recalled his father telling him that, when the different groups represented in Taiwan could talk to each other and listen to one another with respect, Gan Lu Shui should be returned to her country. His father reminded him that she never belonged to them, that for sixty-three years, they were merely stewards of her care. She was not to be donated to Taiwan but returned with humility and an open heart. In a certain light, she became a way for the son to speak with his father, years after his passing.

The wooden crate had not been touched for almost fifty years. Workmen carefully pried open its doors, peeled back the layers of heavy blankets and linen.

Her eyes met the light.

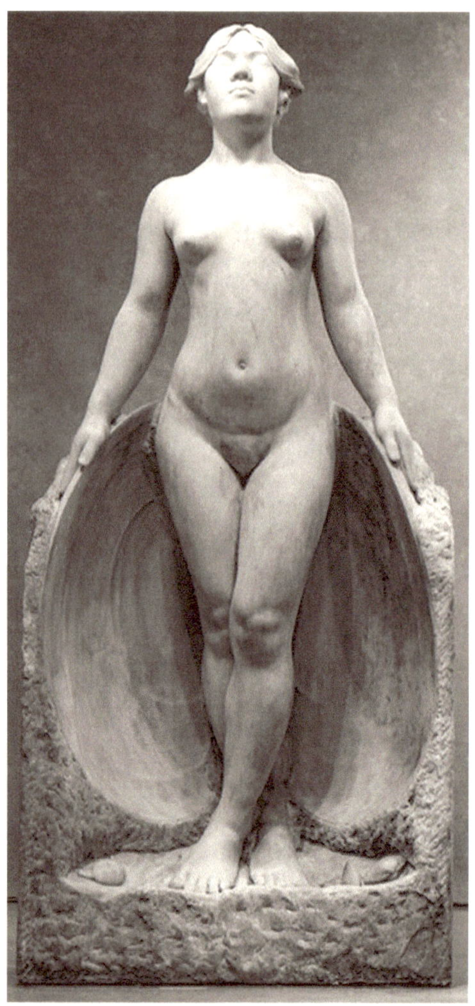

© Huang Pang-Chuan, Lin Chunni

A brief note about this essay:–

甘露水*Gan Lu Shui* reemerged in 2021, exactly one hundred years after it was selected to be in the Imperial Art Exhibition. It was unveiled at the opening of the art show, Lumière: The Enlightenment and Self-Awakening of Taiwanese Culture, at the

Museum of National Taipei University of Education. She was introduced by Dr. Zhang Shi-wen 張士文 ("the doctor's son"), the eldest son of Dr. Zhang Hong-biao 張鴻標 ("the doctor"), who, in 1958, took in *Gan Lu Shui* and, along with his family, protected her for sixty-three years. On that day, at the opening of the show, *Gan Lu Shui* was officially returned to Taiwan.

I attended the opening and was so moved by Dr. Zhang's speech that, when *Gan Lu Shui* was unveiled and I saw her for the first time, I felt something shift. Because I was so drawn to his family's story and connection to the sculpture, as well as to this period of Taiwan history, I followed multiple threads of connection that eventually led me to Dr. Zhang, who kindly invited me to his home in Taichung for a chat. The place where my mother grew up, and where my grandmother operated her famous eye clinic, is not far from Dr. Zhang's home. I spent an afternoon with Dr. Zhang and his wife, Ms. Ruby Hsu, sitting at their kitchen table, drinking tea and eating fruit, chatting all the while. Every now and then, Dr. Zhang would get up to fetch books and photographs to share with me. The result of our conversation is the essay about *Gan Lu Shui,* which is really about Taiwanese identity and art, and which I felt compelled to write.

There is something else to the story, which I did not include in the original piece.

∞

黃土水 Huang Tu-shui, "the young sculptor," was born in 1895, the same year Japan occupied Taiwan. He came from a modest woodworking background, excelled in school, and was sent on a full scholarship to study art in Tokyo. In Japan he was influenced by a European sensibility and wanted to abandon the styles of traditional Chinese art and create a style that was uniquely

Taiwanese. He became the preeminent Taiwanese artist of his time. His sculpture, *Gan Lu Shui,* was the second work of his to be selected for the Imperial Art Exhibit in Japan. The year was 1921, the same year the Taiwan Cultural Association 台灣文化協會 was established by a group of doctors, intellectuals, and artists in an effort toward self-governance under Japanese occupation. Huang Tu-shui was not, like many of his contemporaries, explicitly involved with political activities, but his art spoke volumes. After his death in 1930 in Japan, when he was only thirty-five, his wife brought his sculptures back to Taiwan, among them *Gan Lu Shui,* which was displayed in the provincial government office in Taipei until the office was moved to Taichung in 1958, when the sculpture mysteriously disappeared from the public.

My maternal grandfather was born in 1912 in Miaoli, a Hakka enclave on the west coast of Taiwan. He attended art school in Tokyo in 1936, and though he was in Japan after the death of Huang Tu-shui, my grandfather was considered a contemporary of the same group of Taiwanese artists urgently defining Taiwanese identity through the arts. When Agong returned to Taiwan in 1940, he became an arts and culture journalist for what was originally *Taiwan Minpao,* the only Taiwanese-run newspaper under Japanese occupation. When he had time, he painted landscapes and figures, mostly in oils, in colors that I've come to associate with Taiwanese art from that period—greens, ochres, and rusty reds with a dim quality of light, like an empty room in the middle of the afternoon. Agong joined the Taiwan Cultural Association and, along with a group of artists, formed the Mouve Artist's Society, which prided itself on its freer, more progressive aesthetic. In its manifesto, the artists of Mouve wrote, "We hold a young, enthusiastic and open-minded love for the plastic arts," and in regards to exhibitions, they held little to no restrictions, believing wholeheartedly in the freedom of the artist. For Mouve's first group show in 1941, my grandfather submitted his painting titled *Home.*

In 1944 Agong went into pharmaceuticals, answering the call of family duty to contribute to the responsibility of raising five young children. He manned a space next to Ama's eye clinic in Taichung. The mosaic artist Yan Shui-long 顏水龍, also one of the founding members of Mouve, made an abstract mosaic of an eye on the wall next to the entrance of the clinic. All the while, Agong continued to study and write about art. On the weekends, Agong liked to shop at antique stores and bookshops, buying stationery and books and paintings. When not shopping, he went hunting with friends from different Indigenous tribes, and from those outings, he collected Indigenous art in the form of textiles, fishing baskets, and hunting knives. Agong was always looking for beautiful and original things.

According to a conversation in the 1970s with the artist Xie Li-fa 謝里法, who was an unofficial investigator looking for the then still missing sculpture, Agong had seen *Gan Lu Shui* in 1958 when it was abandoned at the Taichung train station. Agong had seen the sculpture, recognized it, and called on three people: He called on a sculptor friend and a writer friend to come verify that what he saw in the trash heap at the station was, in fact, the seminal sculpture by Huang Tu-shui, and then he called on a Mr. Yu, who owned a delivery company and had a fleet of trucks at his disposal. Agong's intention, as he relayed to Xie Li-fa when they spoke, was to have *Gan Lu Shui* shipped to his home—he and his family lived above my grandmother's eye clinic on Minzu Road in Taichung. Instead, according to Agong, Mr. Yu picked up the sculpture and delivered it to his nephew's home. His nephew was Dr. Zhang Hong-biao.

This account of Agong's involvement with the discovery of *Gan Lu Shui* was published in an article written for the culture section in the *United Daily News* in Taiwan in July of 2002, and when Mr. Yu's granddaughter was interviewed for the article, she contested the idea that it was Agong who hired her grandfather's delivery service, saying that her grandfather was merely doing the right thing by rescuing an art piece, which, at the time, was seen as obscene and cast away as trash.

I didn't bring any of this up in my conversations with Dr. Zhang and his wife, whom I came to call Auntie Ruby. It didn't matter. I was fascinated by the story of *Gan Lu Shui* and how this artwork represented the arc of an important era of Taiwanese history and culture. I deeply respected the way the Zhang family protected her and eventually returned her to Taiwan one hundred years after her birth. *Gan Lu Shui* now lives permanently in the National Taiwan Museum of Fine Arts in Taichung.

What I love most about the story of *Gan Lu Shui* is imagining the children of the Zhang family coming home from school, peeling off their book bags by the sculpture in the dining room, referring to her as their older sister, playing by her side, brushing up against her whenever they passed. Those are moments when cold marble becomes warm, like flesh—moments when art is folded into daily life.

I like to think Agong would have done something just as graceful.

On Collecting
系統

My mother experiences the world as a collector, just as her father did before her. Agong was an artist whose goal was to be at one with all things under the heavens, the Taoist concept of 天人合一, the unity of the heavens and all beings. He understood everything to be interconnected in an invisible and intricate web, and his role was to express that interconnectedness through his art. In truth, though, Agong was not a prolific painter, and there was a large portion of his life when he did not paint. Those were the years when his five children were growing up and my grandmother, who was a famous ophthalmologist in Taichung, was the primary breadwinner in the family. He wrote in later journals, after he and Ama had retired and he began painting again, that he wanted to be tangled in the arts more when he was younger, but, when he saw how much Ama worked to provide for the family, he couldn't. He wished he could spend all day drinking tea, discussing the responsibility of the artist in the world, the responsibility of being a keen observer and of making record of those observations, but he was painfully aware that Ama made most of the money that supported their family, so he couldn't. He wanted to be free to be an artist, but, because he was tethered to the tangible needs of his family, he couldn't.

So, for many years, instead of making art, Agong collected art. My mother's memories of childhood weekends consist in part of going with Agong to the central book-and-stationery store to browse; he would also go to antique shops to buy furniture, tea sets, and paintings. I remember going to museums with my grandfather when I was young and witnessing the way he looked at things—with slow attention, without any regard to those around him, ensconced in his own communion with art. He always carried a small journal and pen in his trench coat pocket to take notes and record observations, to copy words to look up in the dictionary later. This is how I imagine my mother spent her weekends with Agong. She watched him browse and look at interesting things, studying and taking notes, picking things up and turning them around, touching them and feeling their material and weight. And then from time to time, my mother would have watched Agong make the decision to purchase something so that the object could come into his possession. Once that object became his, it must have been like crossing a threshold—of ownership, yes, but also, perhaps, of energy, the energy that moves a thing from one place to another, which for Agong was the result of intense appreciation and desire to possess.

Agong used an antique desk from China, made of dark, heavy wood, to write his philosophies about art and living. He often wrote with a calligraphy brush—slowly and with measure, considering the architecture and balance of each character, leaving the appropriate white space between the components of the word. Later, when he would address red envelopes to us grandkids, he would use the same thoughtful writing process; even if all he had was a ballpoint pen, I could always make out where he stopped in his script to make the turns and angles, where he let his pen pause before lifting it up into a hook. Agong loved to go hunting and often went on weekend hikes into the mountains with his friend Chun-lian 陳春麟, whose wife my mother believes was from the Indigenous Pingpu tribe and thus had many friends who could guide them on these hunting trips. Chun-lian and his wife had four kids, collectively called Bibobuliang, because their nicknames were Abi, Abo, Abu, and Aliang. Agong was enamored with the artistry with which his Indigenous friends made things—their woven fishing baskets, hunting tools, and textiles. Did he buy these things from his friends, or trade them for something in exchange, or ask to be taught to make these things himself? In my mother's childhood home, Agong stored all of his things in a small, Japanese-style tatami anteroom next to the living room. My mother recalls there being at least three to four hunting rifles and hunting knives and fishing poles leaning against the wall of that room, as well as fishing baskets and textile rolls and Agong's painting supplies and stationery and art books.

∞

In 1931 the German Jewish philosopher Walter Benjamin wrote an essay titled, "Unpacking My Library: A Talk About Book Collecting," which greatly illuminated for me how a collector's mind works. In the essay, Benjamin is unloading cases of books during a move into a new space, and as he takes them out of their boxes and places them on the shelves, he considers the memories each book carries with it—the place where he acquired it, the people associated with that experience, the process of collect*ing*, over the collection itself, what he describes as "the thrill of acquisition."

∞

When my mother left Taichung to go up north for university, she felt Taipei to be difficult to grasp; its frenetic energy was frayed, shooting in different directions, unlike the slower pace of Taichung, the warmer, cozier, village feel of central Taiwan. She worked diligently at school, majoring in zoology, but felt out of place. On the weekends, my mother would visit the jade markets, and that was where she found her place, browsing and looking at tables upon tables of jade pieces. She started to acquire a few, and then several, beginning a small collection. Agong and Ama sent her some spending money each month, and she would often run out, having to borrow from her younger sister, who had also moved up north for university. My mother describes the feeling of seeing something she wanted to acquire as an urgent desire, an impulse—though not impulsive. This moment of acquisition was at once calculated, measured, and emotional, a rush.

∞

Benjamin writes, "The most profound enchantment for the collector is the locking of individual items within a magic circle in which they are fixed as the final thrill, the thrill of acquisition, passed over them." The language he draws on is that of sorcery and wonder—"magic" and "enchantment"—it is as if, in the process of transferring an object into one's possession, one is also, at least momentarily, possessed by this excitement. At what point does an object become more than just an object and turn into a thing that has a story, an emotion, even an energetic hum when you hold it in your hands? It seems there is a moment when a collector is taken, almost physically, by the power of this energetic magic, and the only way to close that loop of desire is to reach out and touch the object and hold it in possession.

The act of collecting has always been mysterious to me. I can't relate to the thrill of acquisition nor to the result of its repeated act, which is the amassing of things, often in multiples. How many things, I wonder, does it take to form a collection? Just as Benjamin describes in his essay, my mother is always on the lookout for the next thrill of acquisition—amassing a collection of objects is secondary to the act of collecting, the moment of palpable excitement when she touches a thing that will soon be in her possession. That is the guiding motivation for a collector, who experiences a "whole range of childlike modes of acquisition, from touching things to giving them names. To renew the old world—that is the collector's deepest desire when he is driven to acquire new things." I had never considered the idea of renewal when a thing passes the threshold of possession; some kind of energy is first passed, followed by a desire to transform either by placing the thing in a new context—on a shelf, on a small pedestal, in a glass case, for example—or altering its form in some way.

∞

The first interactions I had with my mother's collection were remote—I was separated from her collection by oceans and cultures and time zones. When my mother was writing her first book on the children's hats in her collection, I was getting my MFA in writing in New York, so she mailed packets of information about her collection from Taiwan to New York. Another veil of remove was language—my mother wrote me in Chinese, and I translated her work into English. This was in the early days of email, so I did not even have access to online photographs and files, only her manila envelopes filled with photocopied printouts of words and grainy, black-and-white xeroxes of photos with my mother's notes in the margins.

The work I did for my mother felt like a chore because it

was something I was doing for her rather than a project we were working on together, which I now know was her intention when she invited me to be her translator. My mother went to graduate school in the United States and worked there for several years before moving back to Taiwan. She could read and write fluently in English—perhaps even more properly than native speakers because she acquired language like an anthropologist, understanding the roots and histories of words, the relational quality of syntax. She didn't need a translator, really. I could have simply been her editor, but she wanted me to be inside the work, to nestle into the fibers of the words and unravel and ravel meaning across languages. I am thinking now about Benjamin's essay on translation, where he writes, "It is translation which catches fire on the eternal life of the works and the perpetual *renewal* of language" (my emphasis). According to Benjamin, the collector acquires new things for the thrill but also to "*renew* the old world" (my emphasis). The collector—and the translator too—desire to breathe new life into a thing, to grant it a new voice and audience.

Still, not having spent time with the actual objects she was writing about and that I was translating made it difficult for me to find the emotional thread that would bring me closer to the subject matter. I spent several more years connected to my mother's collection by this long tether that stretched across physical and psychic space. Billy and I left New York a twosome and moved to Singapore, where we became a family of three, rewinding the length of the tether as we floated closer to home. Then we left Singapore for Hong Kong, where we became a family of four, shortening the tether to home even more, and finally, after we became a family of five, we had pulled and wrapped the string so much that we found ourselves at home in Taiwan, pulled up to shore by this thread. All this time, I had continued to communicate with my mother through the things in her collection—after her book on children's hats, I translated a book on baby carriers, then a book on children's bibs, and then a book on the purses and containers in her collection. While I moved closer to my mother's collection, my role as mother took up more space in my own life. Now that I was home, not only could I physically go to my mother's storage room and hold individual items from her collection in my hands, I could regard them from the psychic and emotional perspective of a mother of three young children. The energy that passed through the objects when I held them was a maternal energy—if there were a way to stitch a cloak of protection for one's children to keep them safe, my mother had collected boxes and boxes of these magical cloaks.

This must be the thrill of understanding.

∞

"Property and possession belong to the tactical sphere," Benjamin writes. "Collectors are people with a tactical instinct."

I used to think objects were lowly and inferior to intangible things like ideas, words, experiences, and dreams. I used to think things were just things. But I am beginning to think that—

things matter.
Things are matter.
Matter comes from material.
We need material for things to be tangible, to have tactility.
The collector's first impulse to possess comes from a thing's tactical quality.
Recalling Anni Albers—"We touch the objects of our love. We touch the things we form."

∞

And in order to work and create shape with material, we need tools. Among the bins storing my mother's textile collection, I found a wax-dye tool.

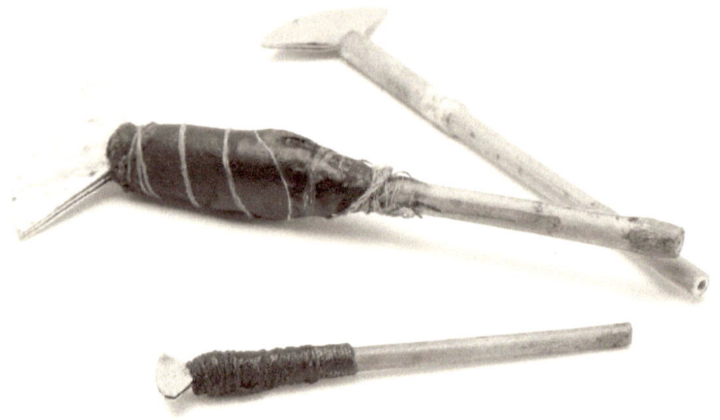

It's made of a hollow bamboo stick and a flattened piece of metal, in this case, a coin. Hot wax is poured into the cavity of the bamboo and flows into the fine edge of the metal. While the wax is fluid, designs are drawn onto fabric. Once the wax is dried, the fabric is dipped into vats of indigo, and when the hardened wax is removed, the wax-drawn designs are revealed as white marks.

On her self-designed textile-study trips to Guizhou, my mother watched women prepare fabric for wax-resist dyeing. They made drafts of their designs using just their fingernails, making linear indentations in the soft fabric, scoring the surface in perfectly straight lines with exact spacing in between. They drew curves without a compass and measured lengths using only their fingers and visual acuity and experience—how I imagine spiders know where to go in space when weaving their webs. There is no calculation more accurate than embodied knowledge.

After laying down the blueprint of a design, the wax-resist dye tool would then be employed to mark the invisible lines, like trodden paths or the fine lines in my mother's upturned palms. The wax is amber, sometimes darker, like rust, but when it is melted and lifted after dyeing, the pathways glow white. It's like looking at film negatives held up to the light, where everything is in reverse—what's light is dark and what's dark is light. How do they know how things will turn out?

As the women work, my mother told me, they hum songs—tunes about the seasons, nursery rhymes, but also songs describing and laying out the steps of cloth making and decorating, which I find at once poetic and practical. I should teach my children songs about how to be, so that they only need to hum a tune to be reminded to recenter themselves when life tosses them up and about. I wish I had a song about writing that I could recall whenever I feel lost or afraid, whenever I feel I need writing the most. It would be a line cast to me—an invisible one, perhaps, but it would materialize into being once I had found a way to come out the other side.

When I first took up stitching, I liked to listen to podcasts while I stitched. Something about keeping my hands busy helped focus my attention. Being able to feel the give of the fabric as I pushed the needle through and the tension as I pulled the needle out, embedding myself in the tactility of women's work, allowed me to be more attuned to the sound of words. In high school, when I spent many hours on the telephone with girlfriends, the first thing I did once they started talking on the other end of the line was find a piece of scrap paper to write on. Writing as they spoke helped me concentrate. Maybe my senses of touch and hearing have to work in tandem. Once, while stitching, I listened to an interview with the poet Jorie Graham, whose poetry I do not understand, and she was speaking about the "vertical energy" of sentences, and suddenly I felt there was a little hook I could latch onto, a kind of synesthetic way of understanding the granular work of writing. Then, Graham said that this verticality must also work with the horizontal line, "like a warp and woof."

But of course! The plane of weaving is the same as the plane of writing —a continual under and over, over and under.

As I continued to listen to this while sewing, I was about to push my needle through the fabric again, when Graham's voice—purple and thick like the skin of grapes—pierced through me. She said to me, "Your voice is the thread in your needle."

From Graham's poem, "Over and Over Stitch": "There are moments in our lives which, threaded, give us heaven— / noon, for instance, or all the single victories / of gravity, or the kudzu vine, / most delicate of manias, / which has pressed its luck / this far this season. / It shines a gloating green."

∞

If not a song, then maybe I could dress my children in clothes that could protect them and remind them of the practical steps to navigating through this world. In kindergarten, children were required to arrive at school with a handkerchief safety-pinned to their chests; the handkerchief would have the child's name written or embroidered near the edges. Something like that handkerchief—a tangible reminder to keep tidy and neat.

"Children's shoes" is a category in my mother's collection. They all have eyes as big as headlights; that way, the children wearing the shoes can see which way they are headed. Something like these shoes too—sewn-on eyes that could help guide my children when they are lost, lonely, or afraid.

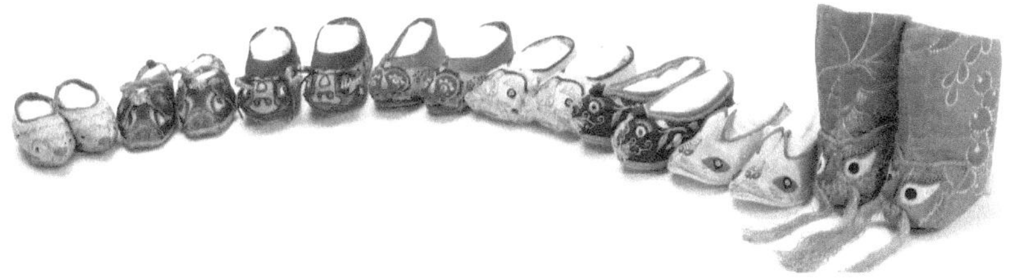

A few years ago, my mother met a Japanese artist, Fumi Furuta, who was living temporarily in Taiwan because of her husband's job posting. My mother invited Fumi-san to visit her textile collection. Not long after her visit, Fumi-san asked to return. She was taken by the entire collection but especially the little children's shoes. Fumi-san had two teenage daughters, and over the years, she had kept their baby clothes and shoes and bonnets. She laid out these items and arranged them into neat rows, then she photographed them; the prints became a series she titled, *The Memory of Things*. The things that her daughters had outgrown were thus reborn into something new—the tangibility and intangibility of the things encapsulated into a collection of artwork. Even though Fumi-san didn't have a personal connection to the children's textiles in my mother's collection, there was something immediate in her understanding of them—the many little articles of clothing, the whimsical hats, the tiny shoes for tiny little feet that didn't even know how to walk yet, shoes that were often embroidered even on the silk or cotton-bottomed soles. What Fumi-san felt in the collection was maternal love expressed through art, but even more than that, she felt and understood my mother's passion for collecting. Benjamin writes, "Every passion borders on the chaotic, but the collector's passion borders on the chaos of memories." Both women—my mother and Fumi-san—have this passion Benjamin writes about, a passion that is ignited by their fascination with memories and their desire to rearrange these memories into a new order.

I also keep a box filled with the special clothing that my three children have outgrown—clothing of first times or that has been given to them by special people, things they wore on special occasions. I see this box less as a collection than an unwillingness to discard. I'm not sure why I am keeping the clothes. Sometimes I fantasize about sewing them into quilts for each child to take with them when they eventually leave us. But for now, that remains a fantasy.

Fumi-san asked if she could photograph the little shoes and returned to my mother's collection on a regular basis. I helped her set up a small space next to my mother's storage room, laying down white paper on the floor and bringing in lights and a stepstool so

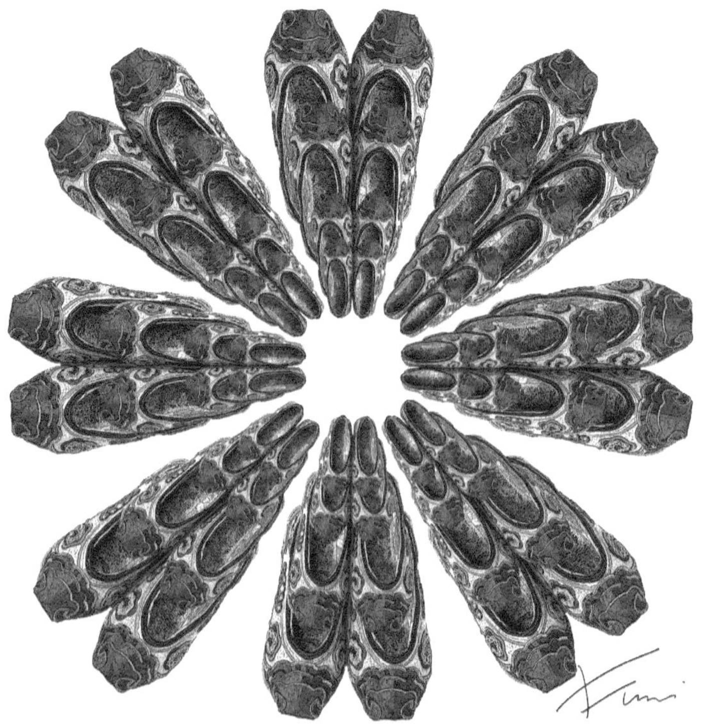

Fumi-san could stand over the shoes and photograph them from above. After a few weeks of capturing the shoes, Fumi-san gathered a collection of digital images, which she then played around with and created kaleidoscopic pinwheels and flowers. These images became a new series of work she titled, *Mother's Love.*

∞

As a child, I was aware that my mother owned a lot of things—ceramic tea sets from Taiwan and Japan, statuettes of Guanyin from China, Indonesian leather puppets, Japanese lacquerware, blue-and-white Hakka bowls and plates, and, of course, children's textiles from China, Taiwan, and Southeast Asia—but I never felt there to be visual or physical clutter in the house. However, my mother has always described herself as messy, and I do recall she was often reconfiguring and rotating her collections for display around our home. This line from Benjamin's essay explained something to me: "There is in the life of a collector a dialectical tension between the poles of disorder and order." Perhaps the mess my mother felt was this tension, which contributed to her constantly organizing and reorganizing her things. When I was young, I would often find her wrapping and unwrapping objects, and when I asked her what she was doing, she would reply that she was in the middle of 整理, which literally means "to sort and arrange systematically and with logic." Now, in her older age, when I ask what she is doing, her answer is most often that she is going through and sorting—整理—her things.

If, as Benjamin posits, the collector walks the tightrope pulled between disorder and order, then I imagine for a collector like my mother, the tightrope inevitably slackens when a current system no longer satisfies, and, therefore, a new one must be devised. That is why the work of organizing is never ending. The reason why there isn't only one system that works is because the things in my mother's collection are, in fact, memories. Memories change and shift over time because our relationship to memories changes—our distance from them lengthens like shadows as the sun goes down. My mother's constant work of doing and undoing her systems reminds me of Penelope weaving and unweaving her tapestry to ward off suitors before Odysseus's homecoming. I am reminded that Penelope was weaving a shroud for Odysseus's father. Penelope was fending off suitors in Odysseus's absence, but, by not finishing the funereal shroud for her father-in-law, she was also delaying the old man's death.

∞

In the last few years, I have sensed my mother's relationship to her collection evolving. Part of this shift is due to my active participation in its caretaking. Now that I am here, now that I am home, I have become the collection's dutiful, though still oftentimes reluctant, manager and archivist. This is how I commune with my mother's collection: I study it; I give presentations at museums and online talks for textile enthusiasts who don't live in Taiwan; I give guided tours and am working with an assistant to digitize the collection in a system that will live forever in the cloud; but mostly, I write about my mother's textile collection (see?). My mother spends a few days a week going through the bins, studying the children's hats, bibs, blankets, baby carriers, clothing, shoes, and tools and adding information about each piece into the digital archive.

I have a sense that my mother is preparing her collection for its next and perhaps final phase. She has told me multiple times that it will ultimately be up to me to decide what happens to it. The collection is still hers—I have not inherited it—but if the decision for its future falls on me, have I just slipped one arm into a coat that has been handed down to me? "Actually," Benjamin writes, "inheritance is the soundest way of acquiring a collection. For a collector's attitude toward his possessions stems from an owner's feeling of responsibility toward his property. Thus it is, in the highest sense, the attitude of an heir, and the most distinguished trait of a collection will always be its transmissibility." The word *transmissibility* reminds me of diseases, though, of course, it also refers to genetic codes that had long been stamped into our cellular pathways the moment we were formed in our mother's bodies. I have my mother's long, parenthetical dimples in my left and right cheeks, the same ones that also framed my grandmother's smile.

Sometimes, now, I will record my mother when she talks to me about her textiles. There are so many things I still need to ask her. Once, I filmed her from behind as she looked at a baby carrier she had collected from the Shidong region, fingering the stitches, turning the fabric inside and out. She was quiet and would sometimes let out a sigh of astonishment, and then suddenly she said, "It's just a kind of crazy." She was referring both to the details in the embroidery but also to her own passion for her collection. Will that crazy be transmitted to me one day? I am afraid. If I don't inherit the crazy, I am afraid I will not be worthy of being the heir of her collection.

∞

"But one thing should be noted," reminds Benjamin, "the phenomenon of collecting loses its meaning as it loses its personal owner." It feels an obvious and cruel reminder to me, but of course the action of collecting stops and loses its meaning once the owner of the collection transfers ownership, or once the original owner is gone. He goes further: "Only in extinction is the collector comprehended." If that is true, how much can I understand and appreciate while my mother is still here, while she is still the owner of her collection, while the meaning of her collection is at its richest and most alive?

Because he wanted to contribute to the family finances, Agong didn't start painting again until his children were grown, but he collected art—mostly paintings—which my mother showed to me throughout my growing-up years whenever she was organizing and reorganizing Agong's things. The paintings he collected were brush paintings of mountains and forests and animals—all composed with sweeping gestures; if there were human figures involved, they were tiny against the backdrop of trees and rocks, rivers and sky. And always, there would be lines of poetry or philosophical musings written along the side or brushed across the top of the scroll. When I was young, I didn't understand the composition, the technique, and I certainly didn't understand the meditative balance that excellent Chinese paintings, such as the ones my grandfather collected, embodied.

Now I understand—these paintings were the embodiment of 天人合一, renderings of how miniscule humanity's role is in the larger web of all life. Nevertheless, the tiny figure drinking tea in the pavilion deep in the mountains is considering his place in the world, the simultaneous beauty and lamentation of ephemerality. There is a line of poetry from the writer, Hu Shih that I remember my parents and grandparents often reciting: 剛忘了昨兒的夢, 又分明看見夢裡的一笑. "I've only just forgotten last night's dream, yet I can still so clearly glimpse the flash of smile in that dream." That's how I remember my grandfather—he was always between worlds, thinking and eating and savoring the pleasures in life, but he was also working for no other reason than his pursuit of something deeper. He didn't need external validation, or at least I don't think he did. When he came to visit, he would sleep in my brother's room. When awake, he would keep the door ajar while he read books, lying on his side on the floor, the side of his head resting in his palm. I would pass by my brother's room on the way to the bathroom, and often I would see that Agong had fallen asleep. As he aged, he would nod off at the dinner table. One minute he was pondering the sushi and teaching us how to eat it—never allow the rice to be sullied by soy sauce, and hold the nigiri with your fingers and turn it over so that only the fish skims the surface of the sauce—and the next minute, his chin was on his chest, and he had slipped into another consciousness. These moments were so brief—but recognizing those moments and now, translating his journals for my cousins who don't read Chinese, I see how earnest my grandfather was about his art.

But that wasn't all. My grandfather passed away at the age of eighty-five. He and my grandmother had lived a full life together, and after his death, we didn't know how Ama would fare on her own, the two of them were so intertwined. But Ama continued to live for another twenty years, past one hundred. She eventually moved back to Taiwan, to Taichung, renting an apartment that was funded completely by the sales of the paintings in Agong's collection. Maybe this is a crude way of considering the appreciation of a collection, but it is tangible and real, and it is ultimately a form of caretaking. His philosophy and his collection of art housed her, kept her safe after he passed.

I hope I am giving my mother's collection its due respect while she is still here. I hope Benjamin is wrong, that we shouldn't have to wait until the collector has passed to truly understand her.

But the truth is, I would very much like to write about something other than my mother's collection.

Interstitial Space

紓

The title of my undergraduate thesis was, "women in small rooms." I had written it that way, all in lowercase. I even used a small-sized font. I wrote my thesis in the basement room of a townhouse I shared with three other women. My walls might as well have been plastered in yellow wallpaper with swirls and paisleys that moved in slow motion like oil gliding on the surface of water. I was simultaneously fascinated and horrified by women trapped in the small rooms of their brilliant minds. My thesis advisor had introduced me to Gaston Bachelard's *The Poetics of Space,* to give my thesis some architecture. The book had titles like "The House. From Cellar to Garret. The Significance of the Hut," "Drawers, Chests and Wardrobes," "Nests," "Shells," "Intimate Immensity." When I was writing my thesis, it felt as though I lived in a house with the female writers I studied—Charlotte Perkins Gilman, Elizabeth Bishop, Virginia Woolf—and I would find them nestled in corners of the house, or I imagined folding paper versions of them into little shapes, tucking them into drawers and slipping them into the spirals of shells.

The radical thinking of the time period I was writing about argued that, in order to dream and think, in order to write, a woman had to be alone and had to have her own space. She had to have a room of her own. Bishop wrote a short story titled, "In Prison," which begins, "I can scarcely wait for the day of my imprisonment. It is then that my life, my real life, will begin." Instead of frightening me, this line excited me. In fact, I pulled a quote from this story as an epigraph of my wedding program: "Freedom is knowledge of necessity." I loved the idea of clean and unadorned spaces, the recognition that constraint actually freed up one's creativity, and the risk of madness from being alone with one's work, one's genius, had a certain romantic appeal.

I pictured time in Bishop's imagined prison as slow-moving and whole, protected by silence and being locked in. It reminded me of the riddle about survival in a room with just a bed, a calendar, and a piano—one could subsist by drinking from the springs of the bed and noshing on the dates in the calendar, and should you want to leave, music—via the keys in the piano—could offer release. The riddle painted a picture of illusion and madness but a delightful one—I'd always thought—especially because survival depended on wordplay, on the manipulation of and change in perspective on language and meaning making. This distortion of reality is seductive because it promises a cordoned space for creative genius. But of course, genius is not something one can aspire to. It isn't a choice. I know I'm not a genius and that I will be spared from madness spiraled and knitted from solitude. And I know solitude isn't a woven shroud I can wrap around myself like a cloak of invisibility because—the children.

But there is also a kind of madness that comes from never being left alone, of always being in demand, physically tugged at, pulled and needed. What is time when it is experienced in constant interruptions, as in new motherhood? Like a record that plays and keeps being spun backward, or a tapestry that is continually raveled and unraveled, time moves in multiple directions—forward and backward, inward and outward, like the backside of embroidery sprouting knots and loose threads, the scritches of the underside stitches. I can still recall the first few experiences of nursing my baby in the hospital right after he was born, of being introduced to a different kind of time in a space that felt immediately adjacent to "real" time; if time were rooms in a house, it wouldn't be the next room but the little closet between rooms. When I was little, I imagined—like many kids—that my closet was a secret portal into another world, but I don't recall spending much time drawing out what that other world would be like. I only ever imagined being tucked in the dark closet with my room on one side of the closet door and that other, amorphously magical place on the other side of the wall. The folded-in space—without a larger context, silent and secret—of the small closet held the greatest allure for me. At first, I experienced this adjacent time when I was nursing the baby, but later it seemed to describe all of our time together, ensconced as though we were within the pearly confines of a conch shell.

The time I was experiencing was parsed into increments, like matter cut in half into ever smaller bits. When we think of infinity, we usually think expansion, increase, vastness, and space. But what I was experiencing was the opposite—or, more accurately, the infinite expansion was happening within the boundaries of each moment. It felt like an infinite series of spliced present moments—time experienced in the staccato now rather than a choral dovetailing of longer stretches and shorter spurts.

In the beginning, being interrupted was both maddening and a relief. My heart withered every time I heard my babies cry and, later, when they became toddlers, whenever I heard them call out for me. I could sense their need—desperate and urgent—before they made their presence known in the doorway of my study, before they placed their chubby hands, little indented dimples where knuckles would one day protrude, on my thigh, pulling me away from my thoughts, pulling me back into the tactility of being. My writing was gluey and unimportant anyway, but then, as soon as I gave in to my children's needs, it was my writing that took on an urgency that diminished whatever their immediate needs were—a book that had to be read (again!), a snack that had to be made, something high up that had to be reached. It was in this tension between the stitches of giving in to and feeling resentful about being needed that I lived in those first years of motherhood.

Living in the miniscule interstitial spaces of time fractures the self. After we moved to Taiwan and I became more involved with the family business, I sometimes traveled to Shanghai for meetings. These were usually extremely unglamorous in-and-out trips, but on one occasion, a friend had gifted me a stay in a hotel suite—a voucher she had won but did not have the opportunity to use. My cousin Ellen, who is an artist from New York, happened to be in Shanghai, so I invited her to stay with me for the night. We ordered room service and wine and talked about the project she was working on, about our parents, about our grandmother, the matriarch of our large extended family, whom we adored and missed. We were in the living room of the suite, and at one point, I noticed that the mirrored wall was actually a sliding door and wondered if there was another room. I walked over and pushed open the large mirror and saw another woman standing in an identical hotel room. I shrieked, horrified that there was an intruder, or that I had just intruded into someone else's room.

It took a long, sludgy moment for me to realize that behind the mirror was another mirror and that I was merely looking at my own reflection. I just didn't recognize it as myself.

Babies develop self-consciousness around eighteen months. You can administer something called the mirror test to check whether they recognize their reflection as another baby or as themselves: Draw a little dot on the baby's nose—with red lipstick, for example—and set the baby in front of a mirror. If the baby reaches up to touch his own nose to feel the mark, then he is conscious of his self. This moment of not recognizing myself in the hotel in Shanghai was a moment of mirror delusion, of not being able to locate the self. I remember it was only when I was able to see Ellen in the background that I finally came to, as if awakening from a dreadful dream, and made out a blurry vision of myself in the foreground.

In *The Poetics of Space,* the house that Bachelard writes about has attics and stairs and rooms and corners, but what happens when the interior of a space has doors that slide open to reveal reflections, a mirrored image of what is instead of what lies beyond? What floats on the other side of the mercurial surface? It is like Alice through the looking glass, where there are vials that invite you to drink and biscuits that alter your relative size. If I were to drink from the springs of the bed and eat the dates from the calendar, would I drown in my oversized tears, burst through the seams of my clothing, or shrink so small that I scurry on spider legs?

Perhaps my brief moment of mirror delusion was in fact a moment of mirror revelation, meaning that what I saw was the collapsing of space and that time was a room of funhouse mirrors instead of a linear path going only one direction. Instead of being horrified that my mind was playing tricks on me, I was getting a glimpse of reality in its true form, soft and bendable, and that ultimately, each marker, each small incremental destination is a meeting with one's self.

I learned how to write in the in-between times, in the interstitial spaces, because that was what I had. I aspired to be like other female writers who wrote about the impossibility of writing as a young mother but did it anyway. I was doing it anyway too, but my language was threadbare, and I was painfully aware that I was merely writing and not writing well. When our younger son was eighteen months, I became pregnant with our third child. Like most toddlers, he couldn't comprehend the physical idea of a real baby growing inside my body; he would lift up my shirt and then put up his hands and shake his head, confirming there was no baby there. Nevertheless, the threat he felt from the imminent arrival of another being who would knock him out of his status of being the baby was real. Unlike our older son—who at the time was four years old and, having gone through this process once before, was too busy with his own growing autonomy to be bothered—our younger son clung to me with more desperation during the day. A once calm and reliable sleeper, he now woke with gurgling screams that I was afraid would jostle his brother sleeping in the bed next to his crib, so I would fly down the hallway holding the bottom of my heavy belly, and when I made it into the boys' bedroom, the younger boy would be sitting up, his little face wet with worry, and I would stay with him, pushing my arm through the slats of his crib to assure him of my presence. No wonder the in-between times I did have in the light of day felt coarse and full of friction, scratchy against the skin. My attention was frayed, split, ugly.

I look back now on the hours in the day when I stayed at home with our younger son while his older brother was in nursery school—how impatient I was to play blocks with him, how overly eager I was to put him down for a nap, how peeved I became when he wet his pants because I was in a hurry to potty train him before the baby arrived. I was a tangle of knotted thread, tightly wound and unorganized. I mistakenly thought that to unravel the knots, I simply needed to locate the loose end and pull, but that only made the knots more insistent, forcing me into tight corners. I didn't yet understand that the trick to unraveling is to soften and loosen the threads, to bounce them gently so that they naturally reveal the spaces between where one can breathe into them, like blowing away pain. When my younger son hurt himself, he would ask me to "hu hu" on it. *Hu hu,* in Taiwanese, which is full of onomatopoeic words, means "to gently blow away pain and tension." I needed to learn how to hu hu on the tight spaces of new motherhood.

When our youngest, our daughter, was eighteen months, we moved back home to Taiwan. It hadn't been our intention, but when we arrived, I realized I was meant to circle back. An invisible string had pulled me home, and once I arrived, I felt that I could see the outlines of things more clearly. In Hong Kong, where we had lived for five years when our three children were all under the age of five, I felt constant vertigo, though I didn't know it until we left and I was no longer suffocated by the dizziness of dense urban landscape. I didn't even realize that the impossibly tall buildings were caving in until we arrived in Taiwan and I could see, wherever I was in Taipei, the outlines of mountains in the distance, the assurance that there was sky and I was part of a larger landscape. I started working when we moved back to Taiwan, helping with the family business and, later, teaching—in fact, I had less and less physical time, but I figured out how to untie each knot of time so that it stretched into a small length of string.

I learned how to write in those small lengths of time as soon as I accepted that that was what I had, as soon as I stopped resisting and softened into the folds of the in-betweenness. There was a dreamlike nonlinearity to my experience of time, the way dreams are not necessarily narrative but make perfect sense the moment before you wake. I learned to burrow in the spaces between the knots of time because, if I didn't, the thoughts would dissipate and unravel in that liminal space where everything simultaneously makes sense and is in vivid detail and is also verbally ungraspable. I am again reminded of the poem by Hu Shih, the simple lines marveling at the experience of having just forgotten last night's dream yet being able to clearly discern and capture the smile still imprinted in one's mind, the shadow of reality, the lasting smile of the Cheshire Cat.

I am not a woman in a small room but a woman moving between the small chambers of time. The intimate in-between spaces of new motherhood are maddening and mysterious, quiet and dark like the insides of pockets, where things are secreted and held—sometimes with intention but more often without—and quickly forgotten. Because new motherhood is a dimension of spliced, interrupted time, women's work, like spinning and weaving, has to be easy to put down and easy to pick up again at a later time. One learns the repetitive act of entering and reentering, making progress like a revolving door that inches forward with each spin.

I am aware the architectural framework upon which I've hung "women in small rooms" was written by a man. Bachelard uses references in literature written by men to confirm his metaphors, surrounding the house as a space to dream and create, but he admits to a certain lack in houses built by men, "since men only know how to build a house from the outside," knowing little of the care and "housewifely"—yes, he uses this word—attention it takes to build the intimate spaces of a house from the inside. There is something to this: If masculine energy is the vertical, external structure of a house, then maybe the feminine is the horizontal, interior attention that makes a house a home. The warp threads on a loom set up the basis of a weaving, but it is the weft threads, which run horizontally, that ultimately give the weaving its pattern, colors, and images. It is the back-and-forth movement of the shuttle, the repetitive over and under of threads that create meaning. The loom is the first computer—a memory system based on a binary order. If I apply it to the demands of new motherhood, of women's work in the first years of caring for young children, then the real challenge is how one returns, again and again, to the creative act that weaves between caretaking and meaning making.

When I first read Lisel Mueller's poem "The Fall of the Muse," which describes the devouring demands of a female artist's creativity, the line "She betrays art with life" felt both like a commiseration and a challenge. How could I write and work against the idea that the physical and tangible demands of daily life sap one's creative energy? The tendency is to separate women's work—caretaking and domestic responsibilities—from creative work, to have a physical delineation between the spaces of domestic work within the home and intellectual work outside the home, away from children. But what if I could use one to nourish the other? What if I learned to move between the two spheres seamlessly? Or, rather, what if that movement *was* the seam that held the two pieces of cloth together? That is the true challenge of living a fractured existence—finding the relational quality between fragments, between moments. Who and what holds these patches together?

∞

THREE PLACES

There used to be a space between my younger son's two front teeth.
It's gone now, the little corn kernels having grown, now rubbing shoulders.
It was a space for goofiness,
the gentle whistle of air
escaping through his childish lisp,
little tongue cushioning the serrated edges of teeth.
I don't remember when all his extraneous digraphs went away,
succumbing to the serious hisses of the letter *s*.
Just as,
I didn't know the last time I nursed my children
would be the last time.

There is another place—
the interior bend of my husband's elbow,
the finish line to a game we play:
He closes his eyes and I trace my finger up his forearm and he tells me when he thinks I've arrived at this delicate inner hinge.
He is always wrong.

Here is the trick—
I move my finger, gentle like cotton,
and trace the underside of his wrist,
the blue-green tributaries of his veins.
I move so slowly that sometimes there is no contact, but an intense hovering
and the vibrational hum between the pale underbelly of his arm and my finger
confuses his senses.
Now? he hopes with eyes dutifully closed.
No, I triumph.

On certain afternoons,
when a midday rest can be afforded,
a leg might dog-ear the blanket as I consider rising,
so that I am at once covered and exposed.
Bird conversations drift in through opened windows,
my lashes a screen that softens the light.
It is here,
where the door between dream and wakefulness is ajar,
that I live.

On Containers and Containment

納

Among her children's textile collection, my mother has one category she has always felt was self-contained, that could likely stand alone—a small but complete collection of purses and containers. And just as with most things my mother has introduced to me, I at first resisted the significance of this category, considering purses to be extravagant and frivolous, but as I worked with my mother on her book about the purses in her collection, simultaneously translating and researching the history of purses and containers and what happened within those small, interior spaces of containment, I began to feel the deep and expansive qualities of those intimate spaces, the human desire to hold and contain things.

The habit of putting things in a bag or container has been a practice for Chinese for thousands of years, and not only for women but for men as well. More than two thousand years old, 禮記, the *Book of Rites,* notes that people carried purses to avoid bad odors and used sachets to chase away evil. Back then, purses were like external pockets, and because bags were carried day and night and were virtually inseparable from their owners, they not only served a functional purpose but also became an emotional attachment for their wearers. During the Chou Dynasty (1046–256 BCE), when a girl was about to get married, her mother would prepare a purse for her to wear around her waist as a reminder of the daily teachings of her parents. It is a kind of poetry to design something that holds reminders and tenets for living to hold close to one's body. (What would my mother have put in my marriage purse?) I began to consider the original impulse for the human desire to contain things, and not just tangible things, but ideas and stories and myths and lessons and values. Is it poetry or naivete?

∞

I deeply admire Ursula K. Le Guin's philosophy about writing, the foundation upon which she builds her stories, her worlds. I am particularly drawn to her theory of fiction, which she elaborates in her essay "The Carrier Bag Theory of Fiction." It's based on the anthropologist Elizabeth Fisher's 1979 book, *Woman's Creation: Sexual Evolution and the Shaping of Society,* which posits that the first cultural device used by humans was probably some kind of container or carrier bag to gather seeds and vegetables. Inspired by this theory, Le Guin proposes an alternative narrative to the traditional—and masculine—hero story that follows men who go out to hunt, explore, pillage, and kill and then return home to tell the tale. The trajectory is outward, the tools are weaponry, and along the way, the sacrifices are many. The shape of that story is like an arrow about to be shot from a bow, the tensions alive and quivering in the pulled back string of the bow. As an alternative to that model, Le Guin writes, "I would go so far as to say that the natural, proper, fitting shape of the novel might be that of a sack, a bag. A book holds words. Words hold things. They bear meanings. A novel is a medicine bundle, holding things in a particular, powerful relation to one another and to us."

That the shape of writing can be like a purse—small and compact, carried close to the body, filled with secrets and surprises—feels thrilling and intimate and deeply maternal. To say nothing of our first cellular memories of being held within our mothers' uterine sacs, babies were—across most cultures—held in cloth carriers by their mothers, grandmothers, and older sisters as women worked in the fields to gather seeds and vegetables, or as they crouched by the river to do the washing, or as they stood

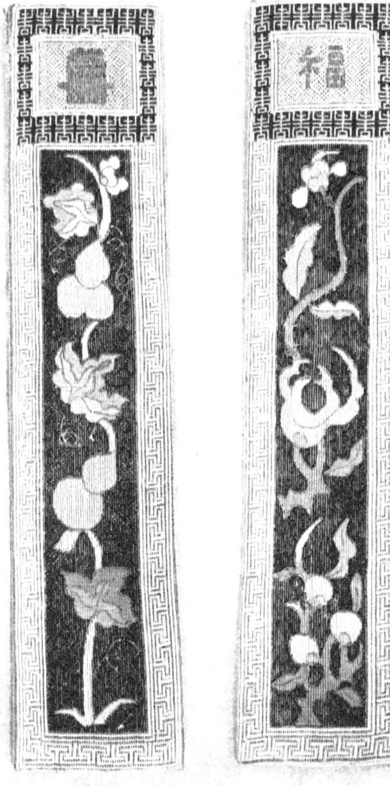

in the kitchen to do the cooking. The significance of the carrier bag as the first cultural device is clear; not only was it used to carry our progeny, our future, it was used to carry other things that would sustain life—food, water, and perhaps most importantly, stories.

I love the idea of a dedicated container for scrolls of poetry and rhymes.

∞

This is how I translated my mother's introduction to her collection of purses: During the Southern and Northern Dynasties (420–589 CE), it was popular practice to gather the morning dew from the leaves of cypress trees, collecting the dew drops into a purse and using the liquid as an eye drop to sharpen one's sight. This purse was called 承露囊, cheng lu nang. There were even purses made to capture mist and clouds from the high mountaintops.

This piqued my interest. The idea of collecting something ephemeral like morning dew seemed romantic but also very practical. Why *not* gather the purest of water? Ancient Chinese people also believed that morning dew could transform a person into a fairy—by cleansing oneself with the droplets formed through the transformation of water from one state of being to another, a kind of metamorphosis would occur. The shape of cheng lu nang was usually a semicircle, and it was carried by both men and women, often dangling from a belt.

Upon further research—extracurricular, because this was not something my mother had written about—I learned of the story about a very skilled archer named 更羸, Geng Ying, whose wife was known to make purses that could capture clouds. Her purses had clasps and could open and close so that she could secure the clouds inside. When she returned home and opened the purse, the cloud inside would still be as white as cotton and merely the size of a cocoon! The thing is, I don't think this is myth. The more time I spend with my mother's collection, looking closely at the fine threads that incredibly come together to form a plane, to form little morsels of hope that I can hold in my hands, I know that there was a time when the portal between the tangible and intangible was wide open and when things and metaphors were interchangeable. I know it because my mother kept our umbilical cord, misplaced it, and then it materialized again. What the archer and his wife used the cloud for once they captured it, I'm not sure. I would use it as thread. I imagine I would be able to unspool this little cocoon of cloud into raw thread, soft and ethereal, that I could weave into the memory of my daughter's warm breath when she used to pull me toward her to tell me that she loved me.

∞

Le Guin: "If it is a human thing to do to put something you want, because it's useful, edible, or beautiful, into a bag, or a basket, or a bit of rolled bark or leaf, or a net woven of your own hair, or what have you, and then take it home with you, home being another, larger kind of pouch or bag, a container for people, and then later on you take it out and eat it or share it or store it up for winter in a solider container or put it in the medicine bundle or the shrine or the museum, the holy place, the area that contains what is sacred, and then the next day you probably do much the same again—if to do that is human, if that's what it takes, then I am a human being after all. Fully, freely, gladly, for the first time."

The human desire to gather the things we need and the things we love and put them into a container, so that we can transport, hold, and keep the objects safe, seems to me now a primal desire and not at all frivolous. We hold things close to us because we deem them essential; they are a symbol of our values. (This thought worries me when I consider that, now, the one thing people hold close to them at all times is their phone.)

∞

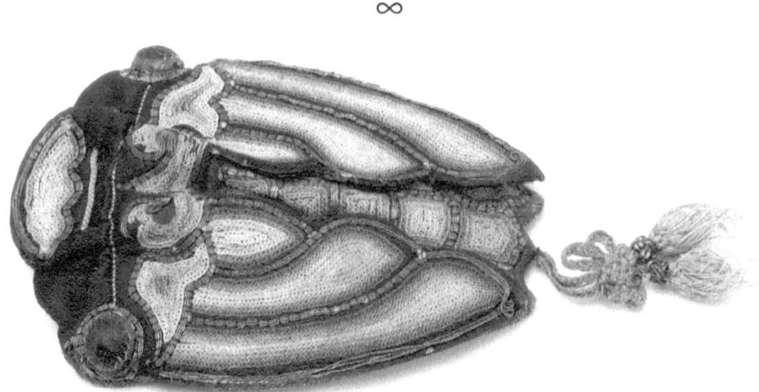

Chinese people are fascinated with animals that metamorphose as a natural phenomenon, seeing them as a metaphor for life. For a period of time, my parents moved out of Taipei city and lived by the river in Tamsui toward the north coast of Taiwan. When we still lived in Hong Kong, before my daughter was born, and I brought the boys to visit my parents, that was where we would stay. My parents' bedroom overlooked the Tamsui River, with Guanyin Mountain in the background, so named because the outline of the mountain range looks like the Goddess of Mercy in repose; you can trace her elegant profile with a finger—forehead, nose, lips, chin, and throat. Next to the river is a marshy egret reservation, where, all throughout the day but especially at dusk, we could see white birds with necks as thin and delicate as a stroke of a calligraphy brush fly out of the grove and into the sky. In the mornings, my mother would go for walks or to the wet market, and once, she brought back the body of a dead cicada she had picked up from the ground, which she wanted to show the boys. The wings were finely laced with Tiffany-lamp patterns, and the body was whole and intact. Something about its construction and its size—so large and easy to study—felt unreal, like it already belonged behind glass in a display case.

The cicada carcass was large, but it was light and hollow, and it felt like the cavity was empty inside and could easily be a container for tiny objects. The cicada sachet most likely held incense or herbs and spices so that the person wearing the sachet would smell nice or, perhaps, so that the aroma would ward off bad spirits. Maybe it was used to carry snuff or an aphrodisiac, maybe even poison. The boys weren't as impressed with the cicada as my mother had hoped, but I feel I understood something about the physicality of that cicada—it was both a symbol of metamorphosis and the very thing that could metamorphose, the thing that inspired metaphor.

For, the shape of a container matters.

∞

Da lian, 搭連, functioned like external pockets and could be worn either slung over one's shoulder or tucked under one's belt. Women might secure theirs on the interior of their large sleeves or inside the folds of their dresses. The pocket was a functional, wearable container and could hold any number of things—a letter, a small mirror, a thin comb. Pockets are secure because they are so close to our bodies; the objects we choose to slip into pockets span the spectrum of importance. Things as important as our money and keys cannot be stolen or misplaced if they are physically on our bodies, or at least that's the idea. We also put things in our pockets out of convenience, scraps of trash or slips of paper that we momentarily don't have a place to discard, and then, inevitably,

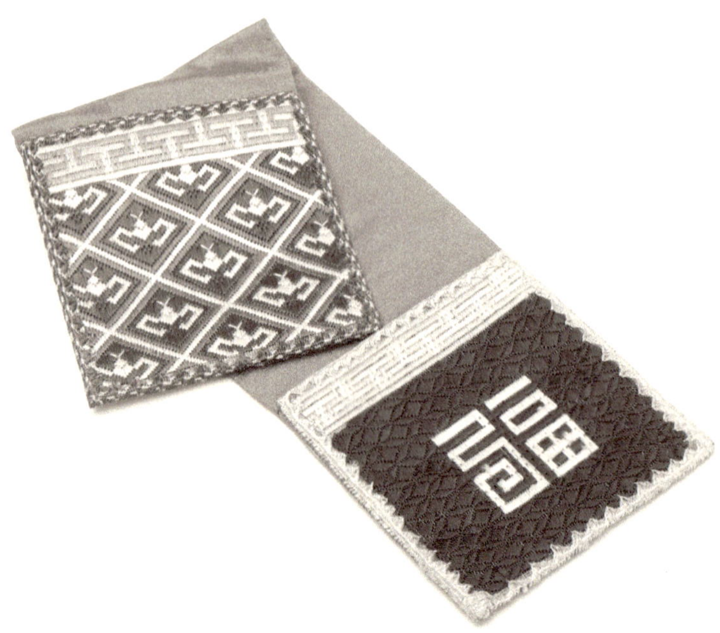

we forget about these scraps, and they get put into the wash and come out mushed together like pulp or moss.

Becoming a mother has trained me to work well in pockets of time—small, dark spaces that are private and invisible. What if I could secret time into pockets to use later, into pockets close to my body so that these little notches of time could not easily be stolen or misplaced? Inevitably, I will forget that I'd slipped these squares of time into my pockets, sliding them into the thin darkness as I press my fingers against my hip bones underneath and sometimes, with deeper pockets, against the very tops of my inner thighs. And when these squares of time come out of the spin cycle of the washing machine, they will be matted and soft like dough, and the words that were written on them will be unintelligible. And finally, the time I had put away in my pockets for later use will be gone, kneaded into bread for the children to eat when they come home from school, always famished for my time.

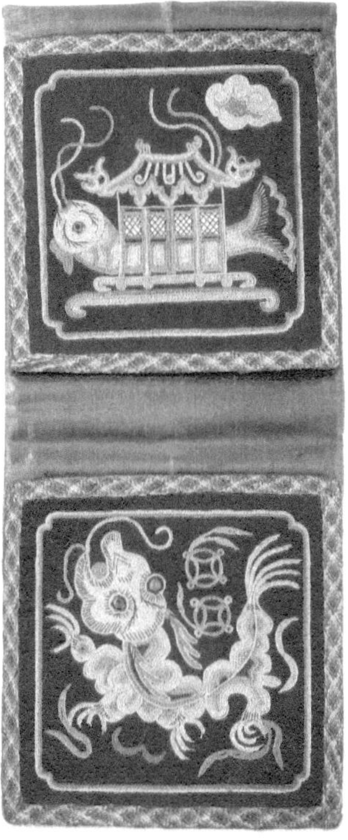

This da lian depicts the story of the koi jumping through the Dragon Gate (龍門). Legend has it that if the koi can successfully jump through the Dragon Gate, then it can transform into a dragon. This myth has been used as a metaphor for metamorphosis, and when embroidered in textiles, it acts as a hope for its wearer to become successful and powerful in life. What fascinates me about this myth is that it is based on a natural phenomenon. Long ago, villagers who lived near the Dragon Gate waterfall along the Yellow River in China observed carp jumping through the gushing water. Astounded by the carp's display of courage and perseverance, they imagined that the fish who made it through the waterfall morphed into dragons on the other side. The truth is, most myths are born from our wonderment of nature—these stories were a way for humans to imagine how and why things are. Mythology is the magic in the real.

When I showed this da lian to my younger son and daughter—they were about six and four—they immediately recognized the story of the carp jumping over the Dragon Gate: It was a Pokémon character—a fish who can evolve into a dragon when it gains power. *Pokémon* is short for "pocket monster." When my children were in grade school, they collected Pokémon cards with a fervor that perhaps can only be matched by my mother's penchant for children's textiles. There I was, trying to collect pockets of time, when I should have been looking to my children and learning to collect pocket-sized mythological creatures, pocket-sized metaphors.

It wasn't just the cards they collected and put carefully into the plastic sleeves of binders meant for business cards; it was the information on each card that they memorized and brought to life in their imaginations. They would spend hours in the afternoon cutting up paper into index card sizes and creating cards of creatures they had birthed themselves. And then they would design elaborate storytelling games with these cards and stage battles and trades. I could join them only in the making of the cards, because it married two of my loves—writing and drawing. I envied the children's freedom and wildness in their drawings and in the creation of each character's backstory. When they reached for a new square of paper, they never hesitated, knowing exactly what they wanted to put down. It took me much longer, and I often had to look things up to find references. When it came time to sit and play with our cards, I was at a complete loss. How was it their little, still-developing brains could remember so much—each detail about every character, the number of hits and damages, whether a card's magic was momentarily disabled because of some special attack, and if another card had just evolved?

I think it's because what they were creating was real. They were still young and could remember; for them, the door between the physical and spiritual worlds was still open. This door closes when we grow up.

∞

He bao, 荷包, can hold any number of things—gold and silver ingots, fragrances, tea leaves, jade pieces, letters, pages of poetry, betel nuts, lipstick. Purses tell such an intimate story of what we choose to carry close to our bodies and the creative materials we use to carry those objects. I am reminded of fashion magazines my girlfriends and I used to read, which would ask celebrities to share the contents of their purses. The purses themselves, and the objects they held, gave so much insight into the featured celebrity's private world. The things they deemed essential were simultaneously banal and fascinating. One day I emptied my mother's purse and did a drawing of the things it held. There were twenty-three items, including: two masks, one folded and one long and unfolded; a small case and the cat-eyed glasses they held; a transparent bag with stickies for electrical stimulation at physical therapy; money and IDs in a small black zippered pouch; two small combs; a foil packet of eight cough lozenges; mints; another foil packet of six cough lozenges; two tubes of lipstick; two cylinders of Rose Crown lip balm, one almost empty; a small mirror; a toothbrush; a makeup bag; a pen; an eye mask for napping; a laminated sutra; a Guanyin stamp; label stickers; and a to-do list.

I would never describe myself as a woman who is into

handbags, and yet I have a section in my closet devoted to bags for different purposes: work bag, yoga bag, beach bag, weekend bag, library bag, reusable market bag and its little sister, the smaller go-down-to-the-corner-store-for-milk tote. Within my everyday bags are little pockets to hold pens, lip balm, ID badges, my datebook, and my phone; I use smaller purses and cases for money, reading glasses, sanitary napkins, tissues, and earbuds. I have small purses for special occasions, passed down to me by my mother. When she was still tailor-making all her clothes from the fabric and materials she bought during her travels for work, she would make purses to match her outfits. Some of them are flat and rectangular, folded and with seams just like a large envelope. Some are round and full, like a baby's diapered bottom. Some are shaped like the traditional he bao, a semicircle with a corded drawstring.

One of my favorite containers is a small, Japanese coin purse that my grandmother gave me. It's red with a repeating pattern of white starburst flowers. I use it to hold my thumb drives, which house all my writing. I carry it every day in the inner pocket of whatever bag I am using, next to my keys.

While studying the objects in my mother's collection, I've learned to see the patterns, and now I recognize the repeated motifs. Whether the embroidered symbols are fish that turn into dragons, or homophones of words of blessing, or geometric and floral shapes that represent life and its miraculous ever-ness, they are all symbols of hope. And because my mother's collection entails articles of clothing made for children, themselves the physical repository of our hopes and dreams, my mother and I started to refer to her children's textiles as hope that one could wear.

One day on my way to the storage room of my mother's

collection, I noticed that the lock on the metal door was engraved with this word in all capital letters: HOPE.

∞

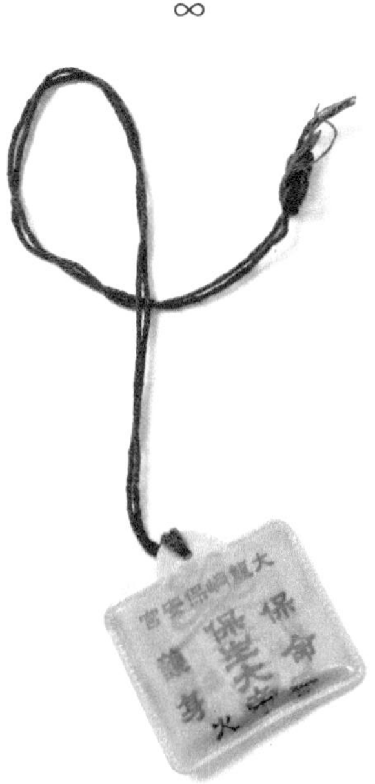

Each year on the first day of the Lunar New Year, my mother visits the temple and prays for our health and well-being. Her prayers are folded up and slipped into a little red or yellow plastic casing, which I tuck into the inner pockets of my wallet so that I can hold her blessings close. The children zip theirs into the small inner pockets of their school backpacks. I love that the children understand that something as intangible and, in some ways, as ineffable as a prayer or a hope can be tucked into a little pocket and held close to their bodies as a reminder of the love that protects and surrounds them each day. When my mother gives them a new one, they hand me her prayers from the previous year. I try to hold on to them, but I've missed a few over the years. I hope they are floating around the minutia and detritus of the children's things, swimming among loose LEGO pieces, tucked into drawers full of artwork, maybe some of them still in the bottoms of their bags, a little flash of yellow in the enclosed dark.

At the end of her essay, Le Guin writes that as a container, science fiction—because that was her genre—has room for all the unending stories in the world and "still the story isn't over. Still there are seeds to be gathered, and room in the bag of stars."

∞

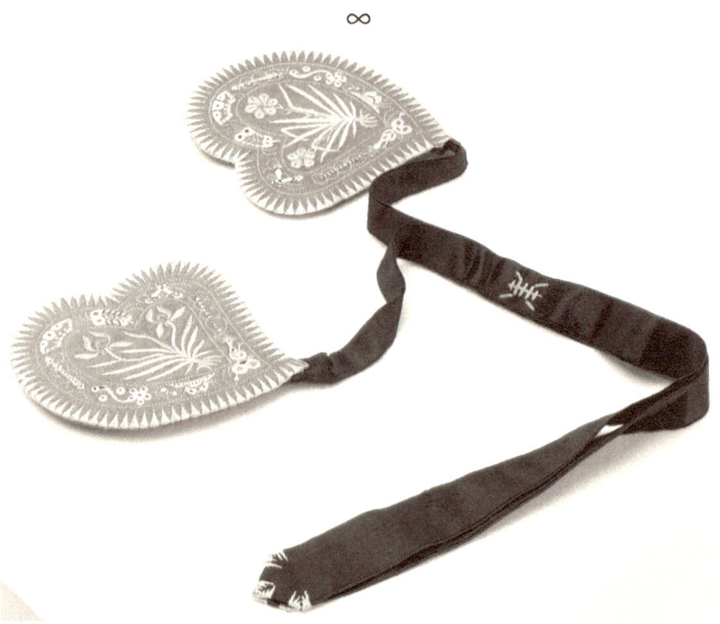

I suppose, in a way, the clothing and coverings we wear are forms of containers that hold our bodies, or parts of our bodies, such as gloves for our hands and socks and shoes for our feet. This heart-shaped ear cover is something that reads like a synesthetic line of poetry to me. When we think of matters of the heart, we associate them with the organ in our chest. I think the ear is an organ that is often overlooked as an instrument that can help us expand our hearts. To listen—really listen—to another person, to the sounds that fill our environment, to the quiet that we so desperately need is an exercise in humility and a radical act of love. My father wears a hearing aid because he is losing his hearing. But it is now, without his hearing, that I see him listening with intention, with heart.

Hearing is the last sense to go when you die.

∞

When my older son turned seven—his first birthday after we moved to Taiwan—he invited the new friends he had made at school to our house. He also invited his Agong, my father. Overjoyed that he was included in the guest list, my father wanted badly to impress my son and his friends. So he found an old-school kám-á-tiàm, 柑仔店, the equivalent of the corner store of his childhood. It is so called because *kám-á* refers to either the containers women would bring to the store to fill with essentials like cooking oil and rice wine and vinegar, or to the large, woven bamboo disks that contained dried goods such as tea leaves or salted fish. These stores also had shelves of glass jars filled with rock candy, dried squid pressed into sheets, round butter crackers with molasses filling, and all manner of toys. In my father's memory, the main attraction was a large carboard box sectioned into rows and columns of square cavities, each holding a small toy. The entire box was wrapped in paper, and for less than 1 NT, children could punch through the paper and reach their fingers into one of the cavities to retrieve a toy. One of the squares held a grand prize—a watch or a sought-after figurine—that the kids would try their luck to find. This box was the thing my father went to the kám-á-tiàm to buy for my son.

My father was right—the boys loved it. They lined up and took turns punching through the paper to retrieve whatever cheap plastic toy was concealed inside. The toy was never the point; it was the punching, the act of breaking through the membrane to access a box that held a possibility, a secret, a small something.

After my son's birthday party, I kept the box, which looked like it was riddled with bullet holes. I tore off the wrapping paper, revealing the squares of spaces that once held the little toys. In a few days, it would be the first of December, so I decided to repurpose the box and make it into an Advent calendar. I put candies and chocolates into each square and rewrapped the box with butcher paper, decorating the outside in a winter theme. For the month of December, my three children would take turns punching through the number I'd written on the box that corresponded to the date. The first year I made the Advent box, my daughter was only two, so she needed her brothers to help her punch through the paper. Surprisingly, the cardboard box was sturdy enough for me to reuse for several years. As the children grew, I filled the cavities with different things—little stationery items, like erasers and small pads of sticky notes—and later, I wrote riddles and fun facts, and I even made coupons for them to use, like one that allowed someone to choose the family movie we would watch on the weekend.

The children are no longer interested in the Advent box, but I still keep it in the closet. It's still clothed in the holey wrapping paper from the last December it was used. Maybe I should fill it with small mementos from their childhood and wrap it in cellophane paper and display it like a Joseph Cornell bric-a-brac box.

∞

In Chinese, "to contain" is 容納 (rong na). 容 refers to capacity; it can also mean "to allow," "to forgive." 納 is a combination of the

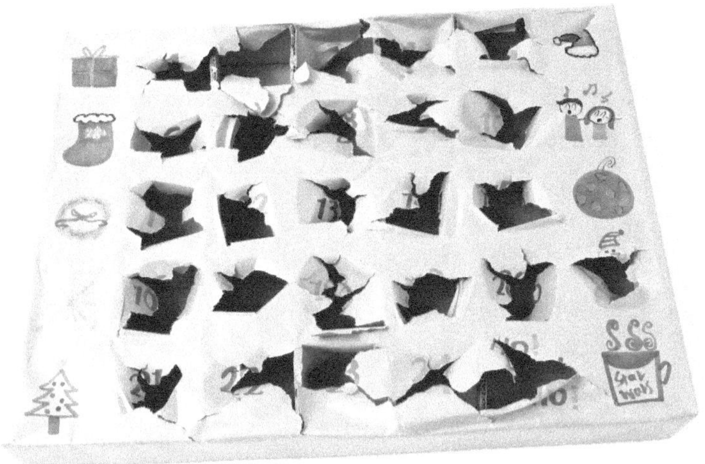

radical for *silk* or *thread* and the character for *inside.* 納 means "to contain," "to accommodate," "to hold," "to collect." In certain contexts, it can also mean "to harbor suspicion or surprise," "to mend."

We contain to hold, to hold back, to control. We contain to separate, compartmentalize, organize, make sense of. Returning to Le Guin's carrier bag theory of fiction, the shape of stories is the primal sack that we—that women in general and mothers in particular—carry, or were once carried in and will one day return to. We are "trying to describe what is in fact going on, what people actually do and feel, how people relate to everything else in this vast sack, this belly of the universe, this womb of things to be and tomb of things that were, this unending story." This unending story filled with the multitude of meanings that the very words 容納 contain—stories of capaciousness and allowance, of suspicion and surprise, of mending and forgiveness.

∞

What I want to do is make a container for each of my children to hold their umbilical cords, which I have been saving for them. But I want more than this Joseph Cornell wannabe box of bric-a-brac memories—I want them to remember that they were once Russian dolled inside of me.

But why?

Why do I continually want to remind them of their connection to me when the job of a mother is to let them go?

Language/Pattern/Writing

紋

One of the best things the yuezi nurse gave me when I was sitting the month at my parents' house to recover from my firstborn was a stack of blank nursing logs that I was instructed to fill in. These are the cells of data I collected:

Date/Time
Temperature
Activity Level
Skin Color
Umbilical Cord
Milk Amount
Strength of Suckling
Spit-up
Urine
Feces
Notes

In the beginning, the information was merely gathered to track the baby's growth and habits, as visits to the doctor for weigh-ins and shots were regular and frequent. But I kept this log faithfully for an entire year, after we brought the baby back to Singapore, where we were living. Billy made multiple copies of an unfilled page and left the stack, along with a pen, on the changing table, which was in fact a cabinet full of books by the baby's crib. Every day for a year, no less than ten times a day, I would make notations in one of the little squares in the log. I imagine that my notations are similar to the pre-language Chinese practice of tying knots on a string to note an event as a mnemonic device. Each notation I made was a certain kind of knot, which, apparently, is all that is needed to jostle dormant memory. I can look at any random page from these logs and recall that day of new motherhood, my stomach clenching into a fist, especially when I see my commentary and question marks of frustration in the margins—"Why won't the baby go to sleep???" I feel sorry for the inexperienced mother that I was, already torn between a desperate desire for independence from my child and wanting nothing more than to be bound together with him.

It is clear that I made these copious notes to look for patterns and to decode each knuckle of time, each small event. If the baby was irritable, I would avoid certain actions. Conversely, if he slept for a long stretch of the night, I would refer back to the hours leading up to it and try to replicate the same sequence of events the next night. One of the first times he slept through the night without needing anything from me, I lay awake, awaiting his signal, my breasts eager and swollen with milk. When his murmurings from the crib came at long last at daybreak, I rushed to him, so proud of what he had accomplished. While tidying things up later, I discovered that a book I was reading but had misplaced was under the baby's crib. I decided to leave the book there as a talisman, certain that the book had contributed to his excellent sleep.

The Chinese character for *pattern* is 紋, made up of the radical for *thread* and the character for *literature* or *text.* Within the folds of the character itself is the spirit of making language material by recognizing the repeated forms onto which a larger shape or design can be draped. The nursing logs I was keeping may not have been writing, per se, but the collective entries created the shape and texture of the first months of new motherhood.

Much like the note-taking stage in my writing process, keeping the nursing logs was an exercise in gathering, in careful observation. In writing, there is the matter of scale—the focus on the miniscule, the words, the sentences, the graphs, on the one hand, and on the other, when to pull back and see the real story, the "so what," as one of my writing teachers had called it. Often, this pulling back doesn't happen until later drafts, until I have spent time away from a piece of writing and then allowed the meaning of it to coalesce in my mind, which very often occurs when I am, in fact, away from my writing, doing something else entirely. This contrast in scale is difficult to achieve when caring for a newborn. Not only is time spliced into smaller and smaller notches, one's body is pulled and kneaded and used for a myriad of functions that, until becoming a mother, it had not been before. The nursing logs helped me connect time and body and notation—they were a very physical form of cataloging, of highlighting patterns.

∞

I found the stack of nursing logs in a box after we moved to Taiwan and the children were in middle and elementary school. I flipped through them, looking at the notes in each cell, and was astonished to find that I could recall the other details of a particular day simply by reading these seemingly mundane notes.

Certain images surfaced first, and then deeper emotions came rolling back.

For instance, the story behind the note, "11:10 tried sling, no go" on January 10, 2007, when my firstborn was two months old, was this: Before our big outing to the supermarket across the street, I had spent a good half hour trying to stuff my baby into a boho-chic cotton sling from my cousin—the one who had gone to Oberlin and gifted me my copy of *Our Bodies, Ourselves* when I was twelve. He cried the entire time as I pretzeled him at odd angles, finagling his last limb into the sling. It was a bit like forcing one too many sweaters into a suitcase and pushing the top of the suitcase down with one hand while zipping it up with the other and pushing extra bits of bulk in with my finger. I was sweating by the time he was "in" the sling, and when I looked down at his innocent, tomato-red face, I popped him free and held him against me and shushed and swayed him and apologized again and again. I felt defeated, like this was proof I wasn't going to be the kind of mom who would be alternative and relaxed. Still, with the baby snug in the more practical and less beautiful BabyBjörn—a gift from couple friends who had their first baby six months before we did—we went across the street to the Cold Storage to buy groceries, and when we came back, both of us were in good spirits because it felt like we had just accomplished something huge, and at 1:35 p.m., when he nursed for thirty-five minutes from my right breast, I think I must have dozed off; thirty-five minutes seems a long time to sit and nurse without drifting off to sleep. At forty-five days as a new mother, I don't think I was capable of balancing a book while nursing yet, multitasking never being easy for me—simultaneously chewing gum and walking probably the most I could handle.

At 2:30 p.m., I gave my baby a massage and danced with him because I wanted him to take a nap, I wanted to set him down somewhere, just for a few moments, so that I could be by myself, in control of my own time. At 3:05 p.m., I laid him down on his belly, which was considered a big taboo by health experts in the West, but I had already observed that he slept better this way. When he was sleeping on his back, his little arms would sometimes jerk up into the air as though he were trying to grab on to something because he was falling backward into space. Plus, the yuezi nurse in Taiwan had told me that, by sleeping him on his belly, I could avoid dooming him to that broad, flat back of the head common in Taiwanese babies brought up by the older generation, who believed a flat head in the back meant a broad face in the front, which was a sign of intelligence and guaranteed high rank. I distinctly remember laying my baby down on the bed in the study, carefully turning his cheek to one side, where I could monitor him closely while I used the time to write at the desk next to the bed. The writing desk was one of the few pieces of furniture we had brought with us when we moved from New York to Singapore. I bought it in graduate school at a nondescript cabinetry shop near the university. It was poorly made, with wobbly legs and two sticky drawers that jammed whenever they were pulled open, but my husband insisted that we ship it to Singapore because it was the desk where I had sat to write my first book. I remember not really writing after setting the baby down but watching him sleep, studying his little nose, and putting my finger under his tiny nostrils to feel his small breath and wondering when he would wake up again.

Focusing on these knots of time was a way of maintaining a sense of control and presence. Making these notes allowed the all-important task of keeping a baby safe and healthy somewhat tangible because there was a visual record, something that resembled a system. Still, it was difficult for me to read through the logs because of the intensity and frequency of its notations, the desperation and judgment in marginal questions like the all-caps "WHY??" when the baby, at eight o'clock in the evening on January 10, was still fussy and not going to sleep. Of course, now I know that a healthy, just-fed baby who is not falling asleep easily is simply not very tired yet. Noting was a way of laying the foundation for order, *order* being the Latin word for the act of setting warp threads on a loom for weaving. In these nursing logs, the weave is so tight, it makes it hard to breathe when I read it, even so many years later.

I didn't want to read the log again, so I put the papers back in the file box where they had been kept the last ten years. The very next day, I brought a bag of old books to my children's school library for a book swap. The librarian leafed through each book to check the condition and take out any bookmarks. From a large cookie cookbook, she unpeeled a yellow Post-it note and handed it to me. On my way out, I looked at the sticky note before dropping it in the trash and was startled to find that it was an impromptu note about my firstborn's napping schedule on January 29, when he was two months old. Apparently, I was trying the cry-it-down method, but because I wasn't anywhere near my official log, I had to find someplace to jot it down.

Or else, what? It wouldn't count?

I kept a nursing log three years later when my younger son was born, and again two years after that when my daughter was born, though the duration and meticulousness with which I kept the log diminished with each subsequent child. I finally did relax as a mother as I became more experienced, but truthfully, I had less physical time to devote to the careful plotting of information that chronicled the baby's hourly activities, while caring for two toddlers and trying to write what I hoped would be—but in fact was not—my second book.

How did the last entry in the log become the last entry? As soon as I decided to end each nursing log for my children, I started keeping a journal for them. It wasn't so much that the notations stopped but that the notes became narrative. I wrote pages describing expressions my children made before they spoke words; they were already wonderfully communicative. I wrote about their first encounters with sand on the beach, the feeling of grass on the bottoms of their soft, silky feet, the sweetness of mangoes, the pucker of lemons, the magic of an automatic door. I wanted to remember *for* them. This period of life fascinates me because it's pre-memory—they will never recall their toddler years on their own, which is astounding, because they are such eventful years. Some of my favorite things to record were observations from spying on my children when they weren't aware I was nearby—when they played with soft toys and made up dialogue, even pre-language; or when they were waking from a nap and I would press my ear to the door and listen to their chatter through the hollow wood. There was so much figuring going on—their experience of the physical world was still so new, and their understanding was immediate, unadulterated by language or culture. I am hopeful that we host at least some cellular memory of this time, nestled deep within the fibers of our being. That my children won't remember the urgency of our closeness in those years makes my heart wither, but their childhood amnesia is a certainty. I don't remember being in my mother's arms as a baby. These journal entries are proof to my children that we were once bound together with an urgent, animal instinct, but, as I witnessed the progress of their growing up into beings apart from me, I reminded myself—and my children in the future, because the entries are written in the second person, addressed to them—that life is also a long process of letting go.

My own journal writing lapsed at this time. Ever since the age of nine, I had been writing in journals, consistently filling a book each year. The impetus, at nine, was to never become an adult who forgot what it was like to be a kid. Over time, the need to keep writing evolved into a necessary habit—it was less a willful, rebellious act to record the state of my being, *now*, and more a compulsion to record, to figure, and, sometimes, just to feel the tactile sensation of my pen moving across paper. I always felt better after I had written in my journal, but what was interesting was that I never felt very good on the rare occasions when I reread old journals—the experience was like drinking too much at a party and waking up wondering what I had inadvertently said that was inane or worse, mean. It's not yet clear to me why I continue to fill journals, but in the years when my children were little, I directed my compulsion and energy to writing in their journals, leaving my own with alarming gaps of six, even eight months between entries.

Those gaping silences, the absence of words, that was something. I was afraid of putting down on the page and pondering these questions: Do my children interfere with my writing? Does motherhood betray art? Even though my journals lapsed, I was working on essays and thinking about continuing a novel I had begun in New York before we moved to Singapore, but the writing was gummy and unsatisfying, like an afternoon nap that the insistent sun ruins by permeating your closed eyelids as you try to sleep. Still, I didn't want to pin it on my children. Even though the attention I gave them when they were babies dulled my own senses and memories, I also admit to the relief of being called away. Some days I was able to feel the joy of disappearing into caring for them. Other days I felt the frustration of being pulled away, but that was still preferable to facing my own inability to think, much less write, with any clarity.

When our firstborn was twelve months old, we decided to put him in a local Singaporean nursery for three hours each morning so I could use that time to write. The first day I brought him to the nursery, my son barreled into the classroom and barely bid me goodbye, fascinated by all the new toys and books and other little human beings his size. Instead of feeling liberated to be with my own thoughts, I felt deeply confused—and a little hurt—by the ease of his transition. I returned to our apartment, just across the street, sat down at my desk, and noted a few lines in the piece I was writing—something I eventually filed under "notes"—but my attention quickly fluttered to other things: recipes for dinner, a grocery list, activities to do on the weekend, furniture we still needed to buy for the apartment. On the second day of nursery, after feeling intense disappointment in myself for languishing the first day, I vowed that I would write for the entire three hours my son and I were apart. But when I pulled my hand away from my son in the foyer of the nursery, where children took off their shoes and learned to place them neatly in the space under the low benches, I felt his little fingers dig into my palm and looked down to find his face buried in the folds of my pants. Instead of feeling vindication—I was, indeed, still wanted—I immediately felt that he must go to the nursery so that I could get to my writing. I pried his fingers back and hurriedly shoved him into the arms of one of the teachers, who, though she was clearly many years younger than I, was much more experienced at handling distraught toddlers. My son must have sensed her calm; even though his heart might have told him to continue to resist by crying and reaching his hand for me, his physical instincts told him it was safe to back ever so slowly into the outspread arms of the capable young teacher. When I left the nursery and rounded the corner, I was convinced I could still hear him crying. I didn't make it back to the apartment that day. I found a nearby café and waited until it was time to pick up my son.

When my children were very young, they demanded my near constant physical attention, and unlike other mothers I observed who could coolly multitask or choose not to indulge, I easily caved. Fine. Okay. Yes, my young children interfered with my autonomy and ability to think and write with much sense. I worked for a long stretch of time as a conduit—of milk, warmth, comfort, and language. I spent so much time with them that I alone could translate their babbles into words. But something was also being planted. The repetition of tasks required by new motherhood—mothers refer to this nowadays as "maintenance labor"—which, at close range, looked merely like notes in the nursing log, evolved into something whole over time. If each notation were like a mnemonic knot, then the repeated series of knots would eventually become a piece of knitting. Taken together, the notes formed a key, the constellation points on a larger star map with direction and scale. These nursing logs, they are the accumulation of all the miniscule and mundane tasks that tether me to this very specific life. For knots/notes to work as a memory tool, we're not meant to unravel and disentangle them, but to figure out how to hold them together on the same plane.

New motherhood is like the process of writing in that, when I'm in front of it, I want to be away, but when I'm away from it, it's all I can think about. When I was walking or waiting in line, or when I was nursing my babies and didn't have a book to read, I did my best, most profound thinking. This is still true now. But, once I sit down to record them, they are often only an approximation of my original thoughts. I can't translate the way the thoughts form, the way they curve and nestle, loop in and out like a Chinese endless knot. Words are never as whole as the embodiment of knowing and of experienced time, but I can't help but to try, again and again, to translate it to the page. There is beauty in repetition and practice, in the magic when notation evolves and transforms into narrative and then into an attempt at meaning. And the knot that I felt in my stomach as I reread the nursing logs or old journals—that knot remains. It is the knot of motherhood, the push and pull between holding your children tight and letting them go.

My very last entry in a nursing log was for my daughter. She was ten months old, and on that day, I had only filled out one row of information (and had left several columns blank even for that one entry):

Date/Time: 10/9
Temperature:
Activity Level:
Skin Color:
Umbilical Cord:
Milk Amount: papaya
Strength of Suckling:
Spit-up:
Urine:
Feces:
Notes: Naptimes—9:15–10, 12:15–13:45

My younger son, who was two and a half at the time, had drawn all over the chart, making his own notes. He was still shaky holding a pen, but his lines were determined, pressing hard into the paper, stopping at certain squares to make his own markings and observations. If I had spied on him that day, I would have seen his big brown eyes focused on his writing, translating what he knew and already understood into notes.

∞

As I write this now, my children are seventeen, fourteen, and twelve. (Writing that just did something to me physically; I felt it in my stomach, a twitch, a pain that is both ache and longing.) The narrative entries I kept for them after the nursing logs have dipped dramatically in frequency. For one thing, I realized they should have agency over what they remember of their lives. The observations I now make of my children have returned to my own journals. When our daughter was eighteen months and we moved to Taiwan, my writing came back to me. At first the writing came in scraps, like candy wrappers I would pocket and immediately forget about. Then the opportunities for fragments increased, and I found I could return to them, like squares of knitting, between my time working with my mother's collection and taking care of the children, even after taking on a teaching job. As my writing returned to me—and it did feel like a physical return, something settling back into my body, both a weight and a capaciousness—I felt less need to write for my children, to log their milestones and experiences and reactions to the world. In a sense, writing for them was my way to step back from the urgent, constant physicality of young motherhood—and by *young*, I don't mean the age of the mother but the age of the children and the time-sensitive sharpness of their needs.

But now, the children are growing up, as they do, even though I couldn't imagine it when they were tugging at me and desperate for me and pulling me away, always away from thinking and clarity. And then one day, I stepped into my older son's slides to take out the trash and found the back of my foot barely reached the divot designed for one's heel, and my toes curled over the edges because there was so much extra space. It was the reverse of trying on my mother's shoes when I was little, pretending to be grown up. In this case, I realized that the growing up had happened, though in some ways, it feels like I've skipped over growing up and have jumped over to growing old.

Moving away from documenting and narrating my children's growing up has shifted something for me. Now I am the one who longs to be close to them in a physical way, especially my sons, as my daughter still seeks our physical affection and pleads for me to stay intertwined with her on her twin bed when I say good night. When our oldest was fourteen and she was nine, she asked me one day why Big Brother and I never hugged. Even writing that down churns something inside—a failure on my part, as well as an immediate defensiveness. Billy confirms it's normal; it is simply that our boys need me in different ways now that they are becoming young men, both of them towering over me, a marvel that they were ever soft and little with tiny nostrils and delicate shoulders.

∞

When the children were babies and toddlers, I tried my best to speak exclusively to them in Mandarin, especially before we moved to Taiwan. I don't remember which language I learned to speak first—I was born in San Francisco when immigrating to the US was still something my parents were seriously considering.

My brother attended kindergarten and brought over friends who spoke English; we lived near cousins who spoke English; my mother spoke Mandarin to us; our grandparents spoke Taiwanese to us and Japanese to each other; and I had a Cantonese babysitter, who only spoke Cantonese to me. So, I can't say which language I learned first, or that there was a first—what I learned was a hybrid, a braided language.

But I can say with confidence that my children's mother tongue—if we define it as the first language one learns—is Mandarin. And it is, in fact, what they learned from their mother.

My Mandarin was fluent and colloquial growing up, though I was never comfortable reading the newspaper or reading for leisure. Its fluidity hardened with each year I spent away from Taiwan after I left for college at age seventeen. I ended up being away for twenty years, so the Mandarin I insisted on speaking exclusively to my children sputtered in my mouth—sometimes it screeched like nails on a chalkboard. I felt shame, even when no one else was around to hear my failures. I relearned how to read and how to speak by reading picture books to my toddler children, making sure I always bought versions with phonetic symbols next to the characters, so that I could read words I no longer recognized. In Hong Kong, I found a playgroup run by a Taiwanese woman who had married a British expat. I relearned how to sing nursery songs and rhymes, and when we did arts and crafts with our toddlers, pasting photos of objects onto construction paper and drawing lines to their corresponding printed names in Chinese, I relearned the proper names of things.

At the time, Billy was working law-firm hours and often traveling, so the children spent the bulk of their time with me. We were learning Mandarin together. I bought DVDs of *Dora the*

Explorer dubbed in Mandarin. Often my days hauling toddlers around the unkind terrain of downtown Hong Kong—on my hip, in the baby carrier, pushing a stroller—felt like a *Dora* episode. I would pretend the errands I had to run or the baby playgroups we went to were tasks we had to accomplish, and I would name our tasks and destinations in Mandarin and narrate to the children what we were doing. When we returned home, we would triumph together, 我們成功了, "We did it!" My life with the children—three of them under the age of five—felt small, only as big as whatever physical space we inhabited at the moment, whether it was our living room, their rooms, the bathtub, the playgroup circle, or a taxi.

Hong Kong in the early 2010s was beginning to feel the pressures of mainland influence, with increasing Chinese investments and wealthy families moving down. There was a strong trend toward speaking Mandarin over Cantonese. Mandarin, in Hong Kong, is called 普通話, "regular language"; in Taiwan, Mandarin, which was enforced after Nationalists arrived from the mainland in 1949, is called 國語, "national language." In Taiwan, the connotation is political, whereas in Hong Kong, it is cultural—referring to Mandarin as regular or mainstream makes it feel inarguable. When I took taxis, I would give our address in Cantonese then continue whatever conversation I was having with my children (usually, I was answering questions from my oldest) in Mandarin. After realizing my address was all I knew how to say in Cantonese, the taxi driver would often ask me to just speak English if I had to give further direction, preferring the language of his colonizer over the language of his dynastic ruler. Within the cramped spaces of taxis, the picture-book, dubbed-over-cartoon Mandarin I spoke with the children made our world feel even more confined and like a *Dora* episode—each section of our day chugged along in bits and increments, and our private language made it even more insular.

On the weekends, when Billy was home, the children toggled back and forth between English and Mandarin with astounding ease. Nowadays, linguists and social psychologists call it code-switching, but after watching young, multilingual children perform it, it appears even more frictionless than the act of flipping a switch. I knew for certain that our children's first language was Mandarin because that was what I spoke to them first, but this was confirmed when I started to notice that they would often use Chinese grammar and word order to speak English to Billy. For example, when our oldest lost his first tooth in pre-K, he came home with a tiny tooth-shaped plastic case hung like a pendant on a strand of green dental floss. The top of the plastic tooth opened up, and inside was his tiny corn-kernel tooth.

"Look, Dad!" He showed Billy eagerly. "My tooth dropped!" 我的牙齒掉了.

Or when our younger son got his first hangnail, he kept rubbing it with the tip of his index finger until the edge of his thumb became swollen and red, and he told his dad he had a "hurting thing," 痛痛的東西, on his thumb.

The rules and regulations of the Mandarin language governed that of English because it came first. But this didn't last. When we moved to Taiwan, our oldest was about to enter first grade, and Billy and I decided to enroll him in an American school. At the time, we felt an American-style education encouraged creativity and critical thinking better than a traditional Taiwanese-style education, which was still largely based on memorization and tests. (We were not knowledgeable about other alternatives and naively operated under the false binaries of either/or, of

East/West.) As soon as he started at the American school, English bulldozed his Mandarin with alarming alacrity and speed—a kind of linguistic shock and awe.

While my written and reading Chinese has improved immensely after moving back to Taiwan, I think my *expressive* Mandarin—if that is even a term—is still unnatural and stunted. Speaking exclusively in Mandarin with my children has become an impossibility as our topics of conversation have become wider in breadth, deeper in meaning, or more technical—as when we talk about their team sports, or what books they are reading for school, or the other activities that swarm the lives of teenagers.

Perhaps because of its diminishment, I still feel an immediate softness when my children speak Mandarin to me. It brings me instantly back to the times we spent together, when it felt as though we were in a cartoon episode built around mini-adventures and celebrations of small triumphs. It was a time when we were ensconced in a world where they were like appendages to my body, symbiotically latched on. It was a time when I could easily scoop them up and nose my way along the silky sweetness of their arms and nibble at their shoulders. When they speak their mother tongue with me, I feel my children return to me in some time-bending, alternate-reality way. And I don't mean in a sci-fi manner, but more in the way the rules and regulations of one language might easily work within the interstices of another language, the way the children dropped teeth and showed us their hurting things, because showing us was all it took to either make something real or make it disappear.

∞

Which makes me realize that I am returning to my parents in much the same way. I have returned to them because I have come back home. I am returning to them through the physical act of caretaking, limited and insufficient as my acts are—holding their elbows when they walk, bringing them breakfast on occasion, taking them on trips around Taiwan with my family. I am returning to my parents through language—Mandarin but also Taiwanese. The only people I regularly spoke Taiwanese to were my grandparents. But they have all passed, and I find that when I miss them, I am also yearning for a language, for Taiwanese. Taiwanese is the language my parents speak to each other, and not just on certain topics or issues—they use Taiwanese to talk about politics, about how they should prepare the fish my mom got just that morning from the market, about the state of our family business; my parents use Taiwanese to bicker and tell jokes and offer small gestures of love. I am trying to learn Taiwanese—sometimes, now, I speak it with my parents. I can understand everything they say, and I feel like I know the response in my head, but when the words pass through my mouth, they crumble. But it pleases them so to hear my crumbling Taiwanese. It always makes them laugh. I wonder if it brings them back to a certain time the way my children speaking Mandarin with me does?

Five years after my parents gifted me the book on Zhuangzi, I picked it up and started reading. It is a book of essays in Chinese by a Taiwanese doctor-turned-writer, who discusses Zhuangzi's Taoist philosophy in simple, plain language. I read very slowly, a few pages each morning, with a dictionary at hand. I also kept a workbook of vocabulary words on my desk. Sometimes, I had to type a character into Google and click on the audio icon to hear its pronunciation. He writes about being egoless, about being one with nature, about the state of flow, but what I mostly got from the book was the simultaneous slack and tension between being present and letting go. In many ways, it's a book about parenting.

I didn't tell my parents I was reading the book. I progressed so slowly I was afraid I would disappoint them—disappoint myself—if I couldn't finish it, but the entire time I was reading the book, I thought of them. I thought of how they were aging and how, often, I still felt like a teenager in their presence, prone to irritation but remorseful immediately afterward. I thought about how they—my father especially—doted on my children in a way they didn't when they were parents and how sometimes that could anger me. But I also thought about how they doted on their parents when their parents were in their waning years, how tender they were with them. And I wanted so badly to be able to be as good to them as they were to my grandparents. And I thought a lot about inheritance and what that means. As I read, I found myself missing my parents, even though they lived just across town.

On the morning I finished the book, I found a photograph stuck into the last pages, something I had absently put there when my parents had first given me the book and just before I had abandoned it. It was a photo of the three of us—my mother,

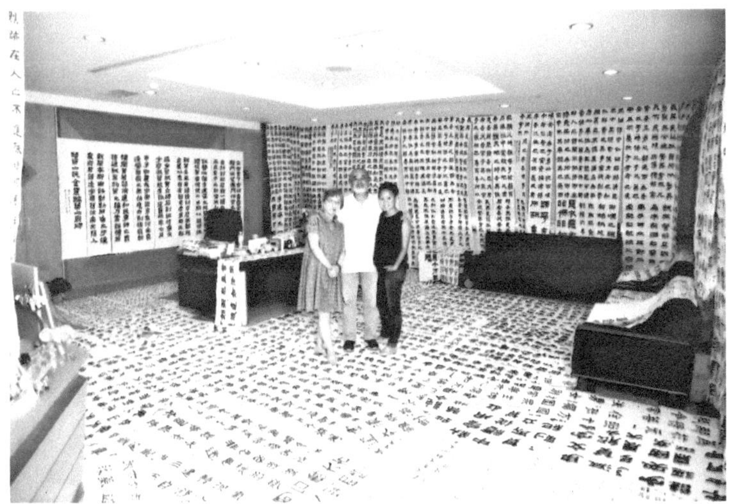

my father, and me. We were standing in my father's office, where he had covered the walls and carpeted the entire floor with his calligraphy. We stood on a plane of white paper filled with black words, all showing my father's signature broad strokes and squat and symmetrical composition. It was the day when he had finished copying the diamond sutra, the themes of which are no-self and emptiness.

Sutra, Sanskrit for "string," or "thread."

My father wanted to photograph his accomplishment before he threw it away.

On Inheritance

My mother and I are in the storage room behind her gallery of children's textiles, the lights dimmed so as not to damage the displayed fabrics with overexposure. The storage room is chilly, made more noticeable by the constant whirring of the air conditioner and the dehumidifier, which are always on at full blast since the textile pieces need to be in a temperature- and moisture-controlled room. We are surrounded by shelves of clear plastic bins labeled "Hats," "Bibs," "Shoes," "Tops," "Baby Carriers." Large reams of fabric on rollers line one side of the room, and in the aisles between the shelves are garment racks with children's clothes hanging from them. Sometimes, when I walk within the aisles, I accidentally bump the racks, and the metal charms hanging off the hems of certain jackets tinkle like the distant sound of children's laughter. Tassels and charms made from metal, grains, or seeds are often sewn onto children's clothing like this because the noise they make is a way to ward off evil.

Currently, we are sitting at the desk, which runs the length of one wall, and we've taken down one of the bins labeled "Children's Clothes" from its shelf to examine its contents. As my mother unearths a child's jacket made of yellow silk, padded with cotton and adorned with traditional Chinese knot buttons, she splays it gently across her open palms. She then flips it around to reveal a drawing of a tiger in black ink. It's not a particularly old article of clothing, nor is it decorated with the intricate embroideries or appliqués of many of the other pieces in her collection that always elicit gasps of disbelief from viewers when they look closely at the handiwork, which was likely performed by the wearer's mother or grandmother. But there's something in the freedom of this jacket's design and the wantonness of drawing directly on silk with a calligraphy brush that spoke to my mother when she first acquired it in Beijing years ago, a relic from the northern region of China. In addition to the tiger, there is a meandering geometric pattern painted along its borders.

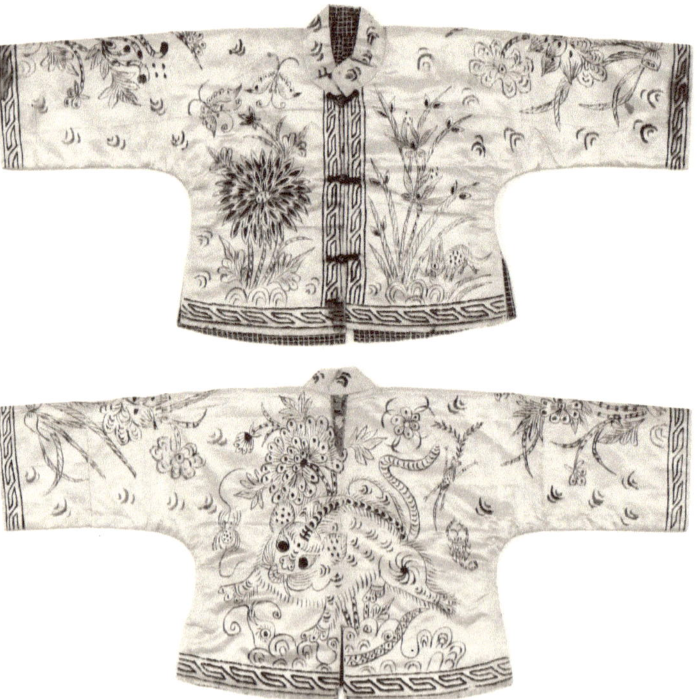

"Maybe this mother was just very good at brush painting," my mother says in Mandarin. "The point is, she didn't care whether or not painting directly on fabric was 'right.' That takes a sense of courage. To me, this is innovation." I am recording my mother's voice and taking notes as I listen. I'm not sure what I will do with these notes, but I have recently come to feel an urgency in collecting them. Already, I have begun to regret not recording my children's voices more often. I didn't know how quickly I would forget the tinny raspiness of their kid voices, the way they mispronounced words, the way my younger son lisped. Or, it's not that I've forgotten, because I can still imagine their faraway little voices in my head—it's that when old videos pop up, their sounds send something electric up and down my body, a mix of intense love and wistfulness. Perhaps it's the same impulse I feel with my mother: It is not enough to simply have a record of her thoughts. I also want to capture her voice, hear its pauses, and make her thinking audible.

My mother brings out another jacket, and this one is large, from the Shidong Miao tribe, sold to my mother by a Miao woman named Pan Yuzhen. Pan was anointed "Inheritor of the National Intangible Cultural Heritage" in China twenty years ago and often travels the world to speak about the traditional Miao art of embroidery. The jacket looks dirty with age, but my mother nevertheless wears white cotton gloves, as she does when she handles anything in her collection; she doesn't want the oils from her hands to damage the textiles. Both its front and back are filled to the borders with an array of embroidered beasts, including the twelve Chinese zodiac animals, an elephant-looking beast, a dog beast, a horselike animal, lions, dragons, butterflies, and Panhu, a being that is considered one of the ancestors of the Miao people. Also embroidered on the front of this jacket is a gate, under which sits a figure holding a pipe. This is likely the shaman who, according to Miao belief, is responsible for guiding the dead back home. The craftsmanship and intricate stitchwork is so fine, I'm sure it has to be from a time before the advent of mass production, which ironically robbed us of the long stretches of time it would take to focus on work so minute and painstaking.

"Actually," my mother tells me, "this jacket is from the 1990s. It was merely made to look old." I look closely at the darkened parts of the jacket, and its sootiness does look suspiciously uniform. I am reminded of a middle school history project I once did, staining paper with tea and searing the edges with a stick of incense to make it appear like an ancient scroll.

"You know," my mother continues, "it's possible this was made to look older to sell to collectors who aren't aware, for a higher price or something. But I know what's going on, and for me, it's part of the charm. I've made friends over the years and have never felt swindled. Plus," she says as she touches the embroidery with her finger, made large and awkward by her ill-fitting glove, "look at this handiwork. And look at the stories that fill this jacket. See how this beast is carrying this young boy? In Miao culture, there is no difference between the real and the fantastical." She repeats this anecdote often, reminding me not to allow our increasingly technology-dependent way of life to close off my view and understanding of the spiritual world. For many Indigenous tribes and peoples whose lives are intertwined with nature, the membrane between the physical and spiritual world is thin or even nonexistent. It is precisely because they live so closely to the earth that they don't forget the magic that surrounds them, unlike the rest of us. For them, the portal to the spiritual world can be opened; this fluidity between the worlds is expressed through stories and recorded on fabric in intricate detail. It amazes me that embroidery—a craft that requires so much time, repetition, and patience—can produce imagery that is this playful and light.

. Though my mother always wears her gloves, I resist the impulse to do the same when I am alone with her fabrics; the tactile experience allows me to appreciate the labor that has gone into each article of clothing, and wearing gloves only dulls my senses. I don't touch the pieces in my mother's collection with my ungloved hands in her presence, of course, as that would be disrespectful, but the next time I return to my mother's storage room on my own, I fold the jacket and put it away in its bin with bare hands so that I can feel the textures of its threads—the satin stitches that fill a large area and create a bulging effect, the knot stitches that stipple the surface. The feeling of its handiwork sends a real surge of energy through my hands—it's as if touch can activate the memory of this work being done, stitch by stitch.

These two jackets are emblematic of how my mother views the inheritance of cultural craft and traditions. She studies the history of cloth-making in different cultures in China and Taiwan, but what truly excites her is how tradition changes over time, how each generation takes what they have inherited and transforms it into something new.

∞

Inheritance can be an awkward thing. My mother and I are in a phase of transition now: Her collection is being passed down to me, but it is not yet mine. It requires a letting go on my mother's part as much as it requires an openness on my part to fully receive it. I have watched from the sidelines as my father transitions out of the family business just in time for my older brother to take his place at the helm; from this exchange, I've learned firsthand how succession doesn't happen the way it does in stories, where roles change overnight. The process is slow and nonlinear, like stitching that needs to be taken out and resewed backward in order to right its way.

The conversations my mother and I have in her storage room are now a meaningful part of her developing ritual of letting go, her transference of stories and memories. A few years ago, I suggested we digitize my mother's collection as a way to archive and index: We took professional photographs of each of the two thousand pieces in her collection and uploaded them to a data-organization platform. I then asked my mother to write notes about each piece—what year it was made, what materials were used, the kinds of embroidery stitches that were employed, what each symbol and motif signifies, and anything about the stories behind each image. Because the pieces in my mother's collection are all children's textiles made by mothers and grandmothers, the images often convey blessings and wishes for good fortune. And because of Han Chinese influence on minority cultures in China and Taiwan, wordplay is an oft-used motif; for example, bats show up repeatedly as a motif because their name shares the same pronunciation as *luck* (fu), so her notes usually contain explanations of Chinese homophones like these. But perhaps most importantly, her notes also include when and how she collected each article, because this is information only she possesses.

My mother spends at least a few mornings each week in the storage room doing exactly this: going through her collection and pecking out notes on the computer. She says spending time with her textiles brings her joy. Sometimes, I join her so I can record our conversations and make my own notes, but most of the time, my mother performs this work on her own or with the help of her longtime assistant.

My mother is doing her part, but am I? Most days, I feel unworthy; other days, I feel indignant, like a sour-faced, ungrateful teenager. Sitting in that small storage room, surrounded by so many textiles—the colors, the evocation of animals, the seasonal flowers, the homophones, all of the motifs evoking abundance and continuance—I toggle between wonder at the material metaphor for life her collection represents and dread of the physical and temporal burden of archiving and caring for it.

The Shidong jacket we examined earlier is about thresholds: the liminal space between life and death, between the physical and the spiritual worlds. I am reminded of the image of the shaman embroidered on the jacket now—how he is sitting underneath an archway, the door between life and death, ready to guide the dead toward their final resting place.

Inheritance is a kind of threshold too, though it is unclear whether it is guarded by its own shaman.

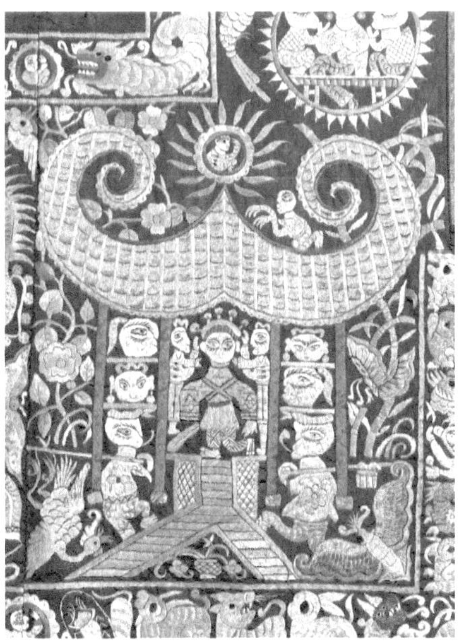

In fairy tales, inheritance is often a central theme; most of the time, it is presented as a reward for successfully completing a test of loyalty and love. A father (who is sometimes a king) with several (usually three) children will divvy up his possessions before his death, and while doing so, something will be revealed about the sincerity of his progenies' love for him. The revelation is usually that the child who is most indifferent to the inheritance is the one who loves the parent the most.

As for my own reluctance to accept my mother's collection, I have been forthcoming about it to her. One of the reasons I suggested the digitization project is because it would make it easier to sell or donate the collection one day. My resistance feels unfilial, proof that I am failing some test. But if—as in the fairy tales I've consumed—a child's loyalty and love of their parent can be validated by their very rejection of said inheritance, or, at least, their diluted attitude toward its priority, then maybe I am a good daughter after all.

Or maybe I have been asking the wrong question all along: Maybe it isn't about whether I *want* to receive my mother's inheritance but about how my mother wants her inheritance to live on. How should her collection continue to exist without her? Does she want me to love it as much as she does? When I ask her this, she says that she has no expectations—that, regardless of whatever I want to do with the collection, she will be at peace.

Why does this feel like a test?

∞

In terms of understanding the kinds of textiles my mother collects, I am a layperson. At best my knowledge can be compared to that of someone who is just starting to learn a new language: They have a grasp of basic vocabulary and pattern recognition but are still lacking confidence and a fuller understanding of the breadth of sentence structure. Even so, I have begun to feel something stir within me, something beyond the information I am gathering from the papers and books—on embroidery, symbolism, and dyeing (its homophone a stark reminder) —that used to take up my mother's bookshelves in my childhood home and that are now finding their way onto my office desk and shelves.

It is a common platitude to say that you cannot truly understand something until you are immersed in it yourself, but nowhere does this ring more true than in the experience of becoming a mother. Within the different stages of my own experience of motherhood, I've constantly recalled things my mother once said or did, particular facial expressions she wore that were cryptic to me in my childhood but have since come to mean something I understand on a visceral level. I now know why, for instance, she took French and Japanese classes in her forties, read numerous tomes on art history, and became a docent at the National Palace Museum: She needed to engage in a multitude of activities to enrich her life, full as it already was from her being a mother and a career woman.

Growing up, I remember wishing she would spend more time at home instead of going out to business dinners or night classes, but now her doggedness in preserving a part of herself that wasn't merely defined by her role as a mother inspires me. Now, in my forties, I find that my mind is also famished for intellectual and creative pursuits that are my own, apart from my responsibilities as a mother. Perhaps most astonishingly, all the little things my mother did in silence to keep our home together are now rendered visible to me—things as mundane as keeping the pantry stocked with her children's favorite foods, calling the plumber when there was a leak, and knowing at any given moment which child's nails needed to be trimmed—because these are the very things I do now. In tandem with these actions, a collection builds from small moments—like changing a sick child out of soiled clothes in the middle of the night or collecting their artworks, writings, and handmade cards into piles of keepsakes for the future. All of this requires a quiet and almost stubborn patience. This is why I don't like the term "maintenance labor," as it is applied to motherhood, because it is so much more than that.

∞

In her book *Women's Work: The First 20,000 Years,* Elizabeth Wayland Barber writes about the history of weaving and the inordinate amount of time it once took to spin and make clothes for one's family. She reminds us of the difficulty in studying this history, which dates as far back as 15,000 BCE, because textile fibers so easily disintegrate over time. In many ways, then, "women's work"—spinning, weaving, embroidery—is a beautiful metaphor for mother's work. It requires time, patience, and a complete surrendering; in this vein, I think of the long, quiet hours devoted to nursing my children. But mother's work is also evanescent, as are textiles—none of my children remember being thus tied to me and, in fact, find it embarrassing to speak of.

Just as inheritance is far more than a onetime act of transference, a mother's work is far more than maintenance; it is like weaving and embroidery, textile arts that require quiet, insistent repetition but that ultimately produce something magical and surprising.

∞

In March of 2019, I helped my mother stage a portion of her collection for an exhibit at the Beitou Museum in Taipei, titled

Stories Told Through Mother's Hands: Children's Textile and Embroidery Arts. It was a streamlined show, beginning with examples of the four "female arts" (weaving, dyeing, embroidery, and patchwork) before moving into the meaning of signs, symbols, and woven folktales. The show culminated with a room full of traditional clothing from my mother's collection paired with modern clothing from our family's children's-wear company. In the adjacent hallway, canvases of digital artist Fumi Furuta's manipulated photographs, inspired by the children's shoes in my mother's collection, were on display. These were examples of the innovation in inheritance my mother was talking to me about back in her storage room. What propels us forward is innovation, but this must first come from a deep knowledge of—and respect for—tradition.

During the exhibition's opening, a simple press event was held, during which a journalist asked my mother which one of her pieces was her favorite. She joked that it was like asking which of her children was her favorite—the point being that it was impossible to answer. But the reporter, not wanting to give up, turned to me and repeated the question. I answered—and this is the honest truth—that my favorite thing about my mother's collection was not a single piece but the time we spent together as she told me the stories behind each and every article: how the things we held came to be, the people she'd met who made or sold them, and where she'd journeyed to acquire them. I reflected then on how mothers do so many things that their children don't see or ever know about, but in this case, I had the rare opportunity to be a part of my mother's ritual of transference and inheritance, to witness our inflection point, holding on to one another before my mother lets go completely, surrendering so I might pick up where she left off and record the next chapter of our story in my own way.

∞

What I don't tell the reporter is that I do have a favorite category in my mother's collection. It is her smallest collection: a series of stitch guides known as 子母花. 子母 means "child-parent" and 花, usually translated as "flower," also means "embroidery." These scraps of fabric are sewn with a woman's library of stitches, which she passes down to her daughter so that her daughter may reference her mother's craft. Later, the daughter will add her own unique stitches to the catalog and pass that down to her daughter.

Stitch guides are the lexicon of a family's history and emotional vocabulary, especially in cultures without a written language. In truth, every family speaks its own private language, but most of us just don't record it. What a beautiful notion to be able to stitch fragments of this private language onto a piece of cloth that you can hold, running your fingers along its raised bumps, reading them like Braille. What if, when you ran your fingers along the embroidery, you could hear the voices of your ancestors?

∞

My daughter has always played with her stuffed animals in a maternal way, swaddling them in little blankets, rubbing their furry bellies, and tucking them into bed each night. Her bed is next to a window that looks out into our backyard, and she likes to push back the curtains to see the moon before saying good night to me and to the stuffed animals in her care.

My daughter is at her most tender in the dark, when we are alone. She likes it when I rub her back or throw my leg over her, putting weight on her body so that she can feel the heaviness of gravity, of our bodies being here, right now. When she has an upset stomach, I rub Tiger Balm on her belly in a clockwise

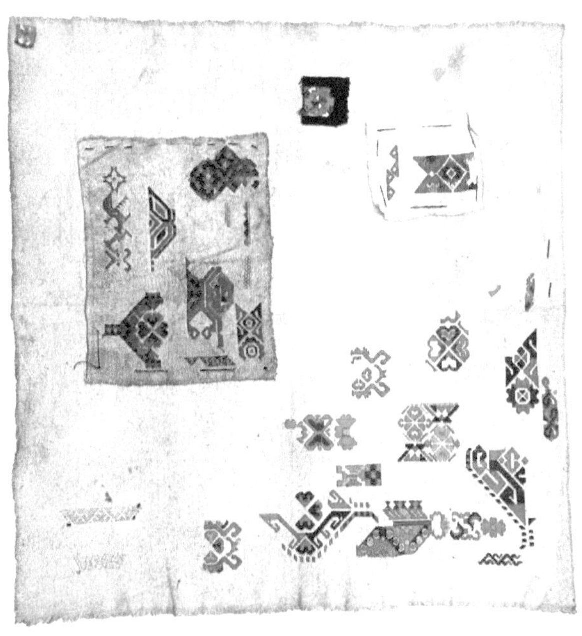

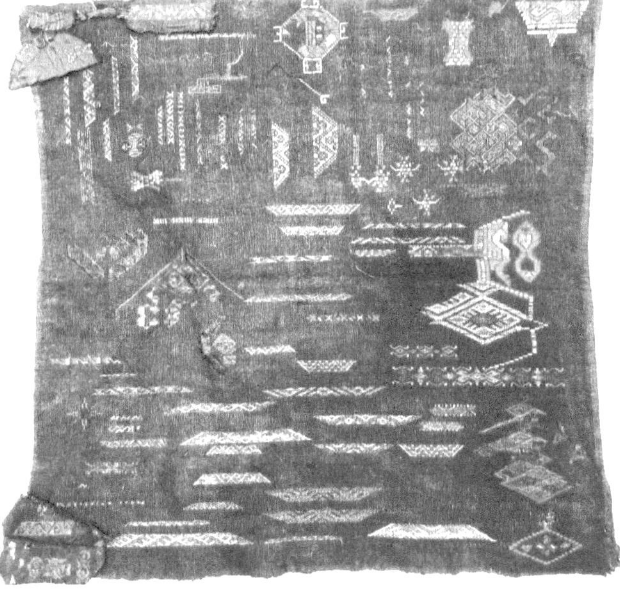

motion to coax out the trapped air. Before turning out the lights, she often asks me to clean inside her ears, putting her head in my lap so that I can swab gently with a Q-tip. In these moments, I feel the weight of her head pressing into my lap as her entire body relaxes. More than once during these intimate acts of caretaking, my daughter has wondered whether women receive handbooks on how to be a mother when they have their first child. I tell her no, but I promise to pass on to her everything I know, everything I've learned from my mother and my grandmothers.

∞

Lately, I have been thinking about my daughter's question in earnest. Should I write a book for my children, or maybe stitch a 子母花? When I first took up stitching, my daughter was about seven years old and wanted to stitch with me. After I taught her a few basic stitches, I gave her her own embroidery hoop and fabric and access to my small array of embroidery floss, which I kept in an old cookie container. The photo shows what she stitched.

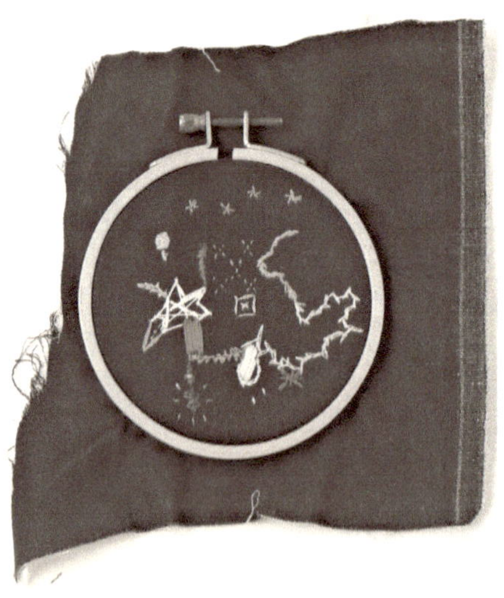

As I stare at the image of this piece, it suddenly dawns on me that it resembles the stitch guides in my mother's collection—it also occurs to me that as I stitch the proverbial (or actual?) 子母花 for my children, I already have one in my possession that my daughter has made for me. Hers is embroidered with all of her embodied knowledge, which I recall from the journals I kept for her when she was young, before she started writing in her own journal every night. I think to myself that I should put this handful of starry wisdom in my pocket and call upon it whenever I am feeling lost.

- ∞ When she was three and we were cataloging things, we were grateful for, "me, by myself" was her number three.
- ∞ When she was four, she told me she knew that after we turn 100, we *brrrrrrr* and become 0 again.
- ∞ When she was five, she told me everyone has three eyes—the two that we see and a third one on our forehead that's used to look into people's hearts.
- ∞ When asked if she wanted to go up to the moon, she said, "No, I like my feet on the ground."

∞

In Lewis Hyde's book *The Gift,* he writes that "threshold gifts" (gifts that accompany moments of change) are perhaps the most common type of gift we give and receive. They are gifts that punctuate specific milestones in the cycle of life such as birth, graduation, and marriage; they have "two sides to each exchange and to each transformation: on the one hand, the person approaching a new station in life is invested with gifts that carry the new identity; on the other hand, some older person—the donor who is leaving that stage of life—dis-invests himself of an old identity by bestowing these same gifts upon the young." In this way, inheritance is the ultimate threshold gift, as one has to pass through the final stage of life—death—in order for their heir to fully possess that inheritance.

Hyde also writes that one of the essential properties of a gift is that it must remain in motion, either by changing hands or through consumption, so that it also changes property and energy. It stands to reason, then, that inheritance must be among those gifts that move most dramatically: It passes from one generation to the next as the giver moves from one realm into another, from the physical into the spiritual.

∞

The Chinese character for *inherit* is made up of five knots:

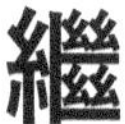

The radical for thread is on the left: 糸. On the right, there are four smaller knots, 幺, nestled in a structure that might resemble a loom. A horizontal line marks a break between the top two and bottom two knots, suggesting that in order for something to continue, it must first be cut off.

I am then reminded that "to continue" in Mandarin is 繼續, which is the character for *inherit* followed by the character for *connect.* 續 also bears the radical for *thread* because in its original meaning, it was used to describe rope or threads that could be linked. I am astounded when I notice that next to the *thread* radical is the character "to sell." Is this a sign—a directive embedded within the text?

Or perhaps, the line in the tiny loom in 繼 can be seen as the threshold between the physical and spiritual realms—the swinging door that infuses an inheritance with the movement and energy Hyde describes as the essential property gifts possess in order to retain their value and meaning. I recall the embroidered shamans on the Shidong jacket, whose figures inspired me to wonder about shamans of inheritance. I hold an image of it next to the hoop of my daughter's stitching.

And suddenly, I see it: At the threshold of inheritance, there are, in fact, two guides—the giver and the heir. It is my mother and me together in her storage room; she is talking, and I am listening as our fingers move along the bumps and grooves of embroidered threads, feeling our way together, just as, every day, I hand my daughter a tiny star of maternal experience for her to sew into her stitch guide—because the only reason I know how to be a mother is because I am a mother to her.

I don't know whether we will continue the work of archiving the collection, sell it, or give it away. Inheritance is so much more than the material thing being passed on. It is the cumulative time my mother spent gathering each object of love, it is my translation of her collection through writing, it is my daughter's stitch guide. Right now, I'm uncertain how my mother and I will emerge from her storage room—but when the time comes, we will both know.

Mao Dun Things

結

My mother talks to me in fruits and vegetables.

On Tuesdays, the first day of the week traditional wet markets are opened in Taiwan, red-and-white striped plastic bags will appear in my house, couriered across town by my mother's faithful driver/handyman. The bags will be filled with all my children's favorite foods.

Even though Billy and I have been together for more than twenty-five years and we can officially say that the children have grown up in Taiwan, now that we have lived here for over ten years, it still surprises and delights my mother when my children like foods that are very Taiwanese. The foods that she sends over include passion fruits with deep-hued purple skin, accompanied by a note reminding me to wait until the skin is puckered before consuming, and small, soft guavas with an aroma so sweet and powerful it perfumes the entire house. Once, my mother observed the children clamoring for calamari rings at a family dinner, and ever since, if she finds freshly caught squid at the market, a bag of three or four will also appear, slick and glistening. If you hit the layer just underneath the translucent skin just so, it explodes into what looks like a million tiny stars. That's how you know the squid is still alive. Cucumbers are a staple, as are sweet potatoes and whatever leafy green vegetables are in season—there is one called "A vegetable" in Taiwanese, which the children find hilarious and will always ask instead for "B vegetable."

On the days she doesn't go to the market, boxes of gift-grade fruit will arrive—giant green grapes the size of plums shipped from Japan or a species of wax apples dubbed "Black King Kong" because its skin is a deep red, richer and darker than the rosy skin of its more plebeian cousin. If not boxes of fruit or intricately packaged Taiwanese tea or nougats or the latest award-winning pineapple or moon cakes, there will be take-out containers of various sizes and half-drunk bottles of wine. Judging by the contents of those boxes, or the name of the hotel restaurant printed on the paper bags in which they were carried, I can often guess the friends my parents dined with the previous evening.

∞

When I first started living on my own in New York City after college, I loved having an almost-empty refrigerator, stocked with only the essentials I needed for the next few days. Once, a visiting friend opened up my cupboards one after another and grimaced while saying, "You have no snacks!" I like having just what I need. This was before Marie Kondo, even before I knew much about minimalism; for me, it just felt natural and made sense.

I have never liked complication or too much hassle. In fact, when too many things start piling up, my insides start squeezing tight, and I feel a physical constriction. In Chinese, *hassle* is 麻煩 (ma fan)—a combination of the characters for *numbness* and *irritation.* That encapsulates how I physically feel when there are too many things around me. I've never named this feeling as anxiety, but I now recognize it as such.

∞

Lately, the things arriving daily at my house have become much more than just fruits and vegetables.

My mother has been retired for thirty years now. She traveled to remote parts of China and Southeast Asia the first several years to add to her collection of children's textiles. She published books on her collection, organized by category—a book on children's hats, a book on baby carriers, a book on purses, another book on baby bibs and collars. She learned about the process of cultivating cotton plants and harvesting silk from silkworms, studied the ways dyes were extracted from plants and flowers, observed the different embroidery techniques used by different tribes, and translated their signs and symbols into stories. She gathered her collection and organized exhibitions at local museums in Taiwan. She did what I imagine I would do in retirement—all the things she always wanted to do but couldn't because of the daily minutiae in the life of a working mother. After the books and exhibitions, she wanted to go on a months-long homestay program in rural Japan to study the language, but in the end, she said my father wouldn't "let" her go. Maybe that's not entirely fair—she did admit to me that she didn't feel comfortable leaving my father, who has diabetes and a heart condition, for such a long stretch of time. So she has been devoting her time to organizing her things, of which there are plenty.

Now, along with the bags of food that appear at my house, my mother sends paintings and lithographs that she procured over the years of travel she did for work. She also sends ceramics from Hong Kong and southwestern China, lacquerware from Japan to hold candies and nuts during the Lunar New Year holidays, and multiple tea sets in blue and white or finished in a cool celadon glaze. A recent box contained twelve stone figurines of the Chinese zodiac, a replica of something from one of the dynasties. By other standards, the figurines could be construed as tchotchkes, but my mother has impeccable taste.

I feel guilty when I complain to Billy that the things showing up at our house make my insides gnash together into a knot. So many of our peers with aging parents have the opposite and unenviable burden of sifting through their parents' things for them. In the end, these are all just things, aren't they?

結

Of course, the Chinese character for *knot* includes the radical for *thread*, and it can mean "to tie together"—as in marriage—but in Buddhism it refers to the earthly troubles that one finds difficult to disentangle from. A knot can simultaneously be unifying and complicating, just as a spiderweb can be both a home and a trap.

∞

When the terracotta soldiers were discovered—an army of eight thousand life-size clay soldiers buried with Emperor Qin Shi Huang to protect him in the afterlife—it made me so sad. To think of all the work that went into creating each and every one of these figures, each one with a different face and variations in armor and accessories to denote rank. There are even chariots and horse cavalries. An entire village created with the sole purpose of being buried alongside the emperor so that he could be protected in the afterlife. Or was it so he wouldn't be lonesome? In my eyes, the foolishness and largeness of this gesture only magnify this sense of loneliness.

∞

I take after my father in my dislike for buying things, and growing up I remember hearing his annoyance over all the space my mother needed for all of her 東西. *Things* in Chinese is *dong xi*—literally, "east-west," hinting at the undiscerning vastness of a collection, everything under the sun. I was less aware of the amount and frequency of my mother's purchases than my father was. Plus she was very good at organizing and putting all these things away—I never felt there was visual clutter in our apartment, and I would never describe my mother as a hoarder. We lived in an apartment building with a basement I never visited; that's where she must have stored all of her larger acquisitions.

I remember three special drawers in her room: One was filled with gifts—boxes of perfumes and soaps and trinkets she could wrap at any moment to bring as a hostess gift; another one was hidden under the trick bottom of another drawer that, when lifted, revealed all of her jewelry; the last drawer—my favorite—was filled with the artwork and poems I produced.

I enjoyed sifting through this last drawer and admiring my own work. One day, I came to my mother's room to do just that and was shocked to find that the drawer had been emptied. She didn't give me a clear explanation for the disappearance of my things, and I accepted that she had thrown them all away, begrudging her this act of cruelty for years. I dug in and indulged myself in feeling hurt, thinking about the way she collected so many things—other people's things—with such passion and scope. The way she spoke about the intricacies of design in the textiles she collected brought tears to her eyes. I, too, was moved by the texts in these textiles, the ways in which language and stories were recorded and written in thread. I understood why she considered the items in her collection exalted works of art; she recognized and elevated the value and place in cultural history of this women's work. But I yearned for a connection to this larger web of meaning; I wanted her to show me how I could also relate and belong to this same world that her collection described. And yet, when I showed her my work, she was tight-lipped with judgment. Once, before I was afraid to be creative, before I began to judge myself, I did a pencil drawing of a tree, which I found rather realistic and soulful with the gauzelike texture of the shaded areas. I laid it in front of her as she talked on the phone with a friend. Later, when I saw she had fixed my drawing with a ballpoint pen, crosshatching one side of the tree trunk to make the shadow more pronounced, I was horrified. I was in elementary school, when I just needed my work to exist on its own as a testament to the innocence of childhood.

Does becoming a parent make you a hypocrite? Because here I am, thirty years later, judging my own children's writing and artwork, keeping only the ones I deem worthy of filing away, of taking up precious storage space in our house, and surreptitiously throwing away the rest when no one is looking.

How does one begin the work of categorizing what stays and what goes?

∞

Often, my mother sends things to the office where I work for the family business. On my desk one day, I find a laminated piece of paper. It is a poem written in Chinese with big, boxy characters—confident in its strokes, the plastic lamination protecting the softness of the pencil marks from smudging. The poem is titled "I Often Wonder" and ruminates on what clouds taste like, how it might feel to scream into the ocean and have the crashing waves answer back, and whether heaven is a quiet place. I wrote it in 1986, when I was ten. I had been wrong about my mother. Being a parent to children who are ages that *I* still remember often gives me a nagging sensation.

After my poem, the things arriving at my house begin to take on a different shade. My mother had salvaged a jade bracelet that broke when my grandmother on my father's side was wearing it. Taiwanese people believe that if a jade bracelet breaks, it was because it was saving your life. My mother mended the bracelet, screwing in some pieces of silver where the hard rock had split and placing the bracelet into a simple frame.

Everything my mother sends to my house comes with a note attached, usually scrap pieces of paper she's come upon from around her apartment, the same apartment I grew up in, in downtown Taipei. Her handwriting used to be measured, the pen making featherlight contact with the paper. Now her script is loose and harried.

One day, a shopping bag arrives filled with different colored silk scarves. They are carefully folded and rolled into infinite folds of pinks, blues, and greens, like the velvet inner petals of peonies. "Most of these are from the '60s, worn by both Amas. If you don't want them, you can return them to me." My mother always gives me the opportunity to reject what she gives me. So, I say yes.

Like any family before the digital age, ours has amassed a sizable collection of photographs over the years. There is one week when little gift bags show up at my house with Ziplocs filled with photos from the '70s, '80s, and '90s, all of them featuring me somewhere on the spectrum of cute, awkward, and cringingly bad. At the same time, my older brother is also receiving collated bags of photos but with him as the focus. After the photos, I receive a small, flat cardboard box, this time without any note attached. Inside is a silver bracelet so small it looks like an accessory for a doll. The chain is connected to a flat pendant with my name engraved on it. It isn't expensive—maybe something custom-made at the local mall in San Francisco, the city where I was born—but it had been immaculately kept, the silver still shiny and untarnished. I begin to feel like I am receiving my life in reverse.

So, it is only appropriate that, next, I receive an invitation to my parents' wedding. The envelope is cream colored, as is the invitation within. The stationery has a feathery, unfinished edge. The writing is unadorned, simply announcing that Christi will be married to Eric at four o'clock in the afternoon at the Water Tree Inn in Fresno, California. The year is 1970. And yet, because there isn't a single blemish of mold on the paper (it comes to me wrapped in a small plastic bag), I could believe the invitation had been printed today, almost fifty years later.

∞

When my daughter was six, she asked me what I would take with me if our house caught fire. I used to consider the same question—it's a good, if morbid, exercise to do to help whittle things down to the essentials.

"I would take 小被被," she offered first. Her "little blanket" with the satin trim that my mother-in-law had given to her when she was born. When she was still a baby, she would suck on a mouthful of the satin edge in order to fall asleep. When she grew a little older, she stopped using the blanket as a pacifier, but she would rub the slippery satin material between her thumb and forefinger until it lulled her to sleep, loosening the fabric into mere threads in many places. Her blanket was the first thing she packed when we went away on trips.

When I used to ask myself what I would bring, the answer was always my journals. Of course, now that I've been writing consistently for over thirty years and have a trunk filled with leather-bound notebooks, it would be incredibly impractical to lug this trunk while a roaring fire chased after me. But hypothetical fire notwithstanding, what *is* my plan for these journals?

My mother wants to burn hers. She tells me this over lunch, which startles me and makes me feel afraid. I ask if I could read them before she destroys them. She doesn't hesitate before saying no. Her resolve is unnerving. Would I allow anyone to read mine? This reminds me of the baby carriers in my mother's collection, how, in some tribes, the mothers will burn them in elaborate rituals as a way to protect the grown child's spirit. So, burning my mother's journals doesn't need to be seen as a severing or a destruction of history but, rather, as a transformation, a passing on. The recordings that my mother is specifically talking about getting rid of chronicle the times when she was resentful and confused and angry. She was uncomfortable rereading them, having them exist. If she could cremate those words, they would spark and hiss, change form, but they would not cease to exist.

∞

I will change my answer to the fire question. All those words in my journals, the handwriting evolving over time, the letters tumbling over each other, falling down, floating up with heat—the physics of them doesn't matter. I have eaten them all.

∞

Most Chinese phrases and idioms are explained by a story. The first book I wrote, which I had dedicated to my mother, began with a phrase, 矛盾 (mao dun). The story goes like this:

A long time ago, there was a street vendor who hollered loudly on corners to advertise his products. He sold only two things: mao (spears) and dun (shields).

"Come, everyone!" the vendor yelled earnestly. "Come and buy my mao! These are the best you will ever find because my mao can spear through anything!" He paused. Then he said, "And you won't believe the superior quality of my dun! These are the most powerful dun; nothing in the world could ever pierce through them!"

A passerby who heard the vendor's cries stopped before him and asked, "What would happen if you took your mao to your dun?"

∞

I write my journals using invisible ink. It's not actually invisible when I write, but the ink dissipates in the heat. I discovered this when I spilled water on one of my journals and took a hairdryer to it, blowing hot air on the soggy pages. Under the heat, the paper went from being soft and wrinkled to crackly and stiff, but as the paper dried, my words disappeared before my eyes. The erasable pens I use to write in my journals are called friction pens. There is a small, translucent rubber nub on one end of the pen that acts like an eraser. It was only in this moment, as I watched my words evaporate, that I realized it is the heat caused by the friction from rubbing that disappears the ink. If I lay my journal with its pages open in the sun, the words will eventually vanish. After this incident, I considered using a different kind of pen for writing. But it was a passing idea.

∞

I still feel numbness and irritation when things arrive at my house, but I've stopped resisting. I file and put them away. I devote drawers and corners of the house—places my children and even my husband don't know exist—to these things. I slip them into the dark folds of purses and pockets. I spin a single strand of silk around each thing, cocooning them into tiny clouds. One day, I will pass them on.

Or let them unravel.

Acknowledgments

This book took ten years to complete. Most of the time, I didn't know it was a book. I knew only that I was seeing strands of stories in the repetitions and patterns between my mother's textile collection and my early days of motherhood and that I needed to work through those connections by writing. The figuring and weaving happened in dark pockets of my mind, and it would have appeared to an outside observer that, when I did sit down to write in the early mornings while my husband and children were still cocooned in sleep, I was alone. But in fact, I was able to work on this book only because I was buoyed by the support and love of many individuals and communities.

Thank you, Catherine Kapphahn and Elizabeth Seay, my original graduate school writing group, whose friendship and guidance has continued through twenty-five years of dramatic life changes. Thank you, Doreen Wang—poet, storyteller, dancer, game developer—whose insight on large portions of this book I leaned on and learned from. Thank you, Cassy Lee, for four years of regular creative check-ins and conversations about art making and motherhood. Thank you, members of the Writing Space, whose commitment to writing together has taught me that community can be nurtured in small and quiet ways. Thank you, members of the Bitten Path—Jenna Tang, Lya An Shaffer, Lilian Huang, and Evian Yiyun Pan—with whom I hope to continue discussing the art of literary translation and highlighting literature from the myriads of Chinese languages for a wider readership. Thank you, Apyang Imiq, who gave me the honor of translating his writing, through which I learned that the work of homecoming requires both physical and linguistic labor.

Some of the essays in this book have previously been published in *Fourth Genre, No Man Is an Island, Seventh Wave, TaiwaneseAmerican.org*, and *WSQ*. I am grateful to the editors of these esteemed publications for their generosity in giving space to early versions of these essays and allowing me to see that these essays could be stitched together. Thank you to the editing and marketing team at the Ohio State University Press and Mad Creek Books for gently shepherding me through the process of making this book material. Special thanks to Joyce Chen and Briana Gwin of *Seventh Wave*, whose profoundly thoughtful suggestions changed my relationship to the editing process entirely. Thank you, Lidia Yuknavitch, for spending time with the manuscript and offering poignant questions and portals for me to burrow my way into the revision journey. Thank you, Grace Loh Prasad, for the Tin House workshop that opened me to the different possibilities of creative nonfiction and for invaluable advice on the publishing process. Thank you, Shawna Yang Ryan, for visiting Gan Lu Shui and envisioning her future chapters.

Thank you, A-mei, my mother's longtime textile collection assistant, whose devotion to the study, categorization, and digitization of the collection has deepened our understanding of the stories embedded within the collection—piece by piece but also together, as a whole.

Thank you, Mom, for giving me the central metaphor of my adult writing life—text and textiles. Thank you, Dad, for modeling the discipline of daily practice and for the delight, these past ten years, of gifting me a word each year. Thank you, Alex, for never wavering from the most important thing that grounds us all—love and devotion to family.

To my three children, whom I love "in a circle," thank you for teaching me how to be brave.

And finally, thank you, Billy, always my first and best reader, with whom I am blessed to share this cocoon, and for whom I write each word.

The Journal Non/Fiction Prize
(formerly The Ohio State University Prize in Short Fiction)

Unraveling Threads: Essays on Inheritance
BRENDA LIN

My Prisoner and Other Stories
TYLER MCANDREW

The Registry of Forgotten Objects: Stories
MILES HARVEY

Zoo World: Essays
MARY QUADE

Our Sister Who Will Not Die: Stories
REBECCA BERNARD

The Age of Discovery and Other Stories
BECKY HAGENSTON

Sign Here If You Exist and Other Essays
JILL SISSON QUINN

When: Stories
KATHERINE ZLABEK

Out of Step: A Memoir
ANTHONY MOLL

Brief Interviews with the Romantic Past
KATHRYN NUERNBERGER

Landfall: A Ring of Stories
JULIE HENSLEY

Hibernate
ELIZABETH ESLAMI

The Deer in the Mirror
CARY HOLLADAY

How
GEOFF WYSS

Little America
DIANE SIMMONS

The Book of Right and Wrong
MATT DEBENHAM

The Departure Lounge: Stories and a Novella
PAUL EGGERS

True Kin
RIC JAHNA

Owner's Manual
MORGAN MCDERMOTT

Mexico Is Missing: And Other Stories
J. DAVID STEVENS

Ordination
SCOTT A. KAUKONEN

Little Men: Novellas and Stories
GERALD SHAPIRO

The Bones of Garbo
TRUDY LEWIS

The White Tattoo: A Collection of Short Stories
WILLIAM J. COBB

Come Back Irish
WENDY RAWLINGS

Throwing Knives
MOLLY BEST TINSLEY

Dating Miss Universe: Nine Stories
STEVEN POLANSKY

Radiance: Ten Stories
JOHN J. CLAYTON

www.ingramcontent.com/pod-product-compliance
Lightning Source LLC
LaVergne TN
LVHW100921110826
845155LV00035B/38

* 9 7 8 0 8 1 4 2 5 9 8 8 7 *